7 Languages
in
7 Years

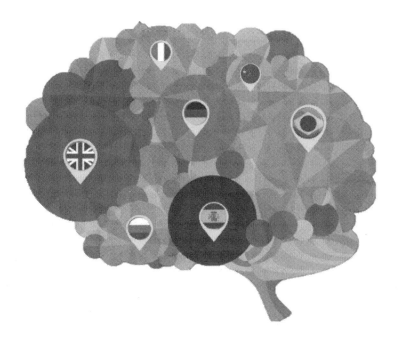

Debora G. Barbosa

Publisher's note

This edition first published 2017

© 2017, Debora G. Barbosa

The right of the author to be identified as the author of this work has been asserted in accordance with the Copyright, Designs and Patents Act 1988.

Printed in August 2017

G. Barbosa, Debora, author.

7 Languages in 7 Years: The truth behind learning a foreign language, and how even the busiest person can master it on their own in 365 days / Debora G. Barbosa. – First edition.

Includes index.
ISBN 9781522004882
Independently published.
Cover design: Debora G. Barbosa
Printed in Great Britain by Amazon Kindle, Manchester UK

Debora G. Barbosa is a Brazilian business woman that has learned throughout the past 6 years of her life, 6 different languages from Russian to German, Spanish, English and Chinese. Born in 1995, Debora has moved entirely on her own to the United States at age 15 to complete her high school studies. Later in 2013 at age 17, she moved then to Manchester, England where she currently pursues a Bachelors degree in Business at the University of Salford. After translating some of the most expensive football players in the world at the young age of 19 for Manchester United F.C. and continuing on with the work for three more years, Debora hopes to assist people all over the world that wish to learn a foreign language but struggle due to lack of time or personal difficulty.

"If you talk to a man in a language he understands, that goes to his head. If you talk to him in his language, that goes to his heart." –Nelson Mandela

7 Languages
in
7 Years

Contents

Preface

Gone were the days where people were satisfied growing up and living their entire lives only in one place. Today's reality is quite different from our ancestors. People now travel more than ever, with cheaper prices and better transportation systems, it is no longer difficult to move around. As we become more and more connected to other cultures, the need to learn different idioms means not only adapting better to the path our society is leading us to, but also standing out above competition in the ever growing competitive work market of today. After years of experience in the learning and using of different languages, I have decided to write this book with the purpose to assist millions of people that wish to learn a different language but don't have the time while carrying on with their busy lives. Or perhaps, they do have the time but not the money or energy needed. After all, how else can anyone learn another language without moving to a different country and being forced to learn it by necessity? The truth is that it is easier than it seems really, if you're determined enough to go through it.

In this book, I will do my best to help you accomplish this goal and change your life for the better.

Introduction

Language not only is our main form of communication with others but it is also a tool that transmits learning and cultural aspects through generations. The main reason humanity has been constantly achieving new heights, is that we as humans have built technologies and civilizations that would be absolutely impossible to do so without the use of languages. The evolutionary biologist Martin Nowak has gone as far as saying that language is "the most interesting invention of the last 600 million years". For him, their impact in our history can only be compared to few other important events such as the evolution of life itself and of multi-celled animals.

In this ever changing world we are constantly surrounded by uncertainties and fierce competition. While some view learning another language as a novelty or something that they will never use, the reality is that the work force is becoming more and more skilled while good high profile jobs are becoming harder to find. Standing out from the crowd is not only necessary but it is also the new rule for those looking to enter the working force and to build a successful career. Although learning a foreign language does not automatically guarantees a high paying job, it will definitely increase your chances of getting one. The benefits that come along the learning of a new idiom are far greater than just a better looking CV. In this book, I will be arguing the best case on why you should be teaching yourself a foreign language right now and how doing this can greatly improve your life.

We are now in 2017 and many people claim on the internet that it is perfectly possible to become fluent in any language within a certain amount of days or weeks. However, for the average person in today's society it is rather impossible to merge busy routines with the time and focus that is required to learn a different language. There is of course for many, the option of adventuring oneself abroad for a certain period of time – which is in my opinion, by far the best choice when it comes to learning another language. However in reality, few of us have the time, the money or the energy to do such things. I wouldn't say it is a lack of opportunity, as opportunities can be created, nevertheless is it worth sacrificing so much time of your life just to be able to understand and communicate in a foreign tongue? For some yes, for most no.

In this book I will be introducing you to my method of learning several different languages through a number of years. We will be looking at solid facts as well as personal experiences to help us understand how even the busiest person on earth can become a polyglot in no time. Let me introduce you to the changes that occur in our brain with each new idiom, and how we begin to perceive the world as a different place. If you have read this far, you should be asking yourself – am I ready to change how I see the world? Speaking a different language means to see life through the eyes of a different culture. Therefore, learning a language isn't a decision you take out of just necessity, it is a decision based on your life priorities and goals. Think of who you are today and who you want to be in the years to come. In this book, I will try my best to guide you through the process of learning a new language on your own – without sacrificing too much of your time.

Before I present you with loads of information, let me share with you a secret that most people don't seem to know – one does not becomes fluent in a language through books, audio books nor from sitting inside a classroom. One instead becomes fluent by fully, completely embracing and most importantly, thinking, into the desired language. It is crucial therefore to understand what is the culture behind the language in particular that you wish to learn. Take some time to carefully research the country where the language is most spoken at and the culture behind the elements of whichever of the current over 7000 languages around the world you choose to learn. This is not a book for those looking for academic sources on how each language was created or the etymology behind them. This is a clear and practical guide on how to teach yourself any language without disrupting your busy life. Enough with introductions, let's get to facts!

Chapter I

THE LANGUAGES OF THE WORLD

"He who knows no foreign languages,
knows nothing of the world."
- Johann Wolfgang von Goethe

In our busy everyday lives we usually take language for granted. However it only really takes a moment's reflection to show how important this is in our lives. In some way or another, language also dominates our social and cognitive activities that it would be nearly impossible to imagine what our lives would be like without them. Indeed, for most of us language is considered to be an essential part of what really means to be a human, besides being what separates us from other animals. Our culture and our technology entirely depends on it. The primary purpose of language itself is obviously to communicate with each other, but it can also be used to express emotion i.e. swearing, to engage in social interactions i.e. greeting people, to record information i.e. birth certificates, and to express one's identify in many forms. As complex as all languages are, their origins are just as complicated and interconnected. Languages are a living thing, they change on a constant basis with the addiction and removal of words, and even become extinct as it can be seen with several indigenous tribes that become smaller and more globalized each day all around the world.

How many languages exist today?

When people are asked how many languages they believe are spoken today in the world, the answers tend to vary from a few hundreds to a couple of thousands. However, when we choose to count them, the number does not even come close. By looking at reliable references, we can see how the number of languages in existence has drastically increased through time. The 1911 (11th) edition of the Encyclopaedia Britannica, for example, implies a figure somewhere around 1,000, a number that climbs steadily over the course of the twentieth century. That is not due to any increase in the number of languages itself, but rather to our increased understanding of how many languages are spoken in areas that had previously been unknown.

Figure 1. 1 Language speakers around the world

Languages   Population

Above we see the places with highest number of concentrated languages – most heavily in Africa, Asia, and the Pacific. But then again how many people do really speak them? Most of the population uses Asian or European languages, mostly due to the years of colonial expansion that have shaped the culture and idioms of many countries. In contrast, Pacific languages – which account for 18.5% of the world's languages – are spoken by so few people that the region barely even registers on the population graphic above. Countries such as Dagestan located in the Caucasus inside Russian Federation, have over 100 different languages actively spoken while in India it is believed that over 1,000 dialects and languages are currently used.

Much pioneering work in documenting the languages of the world has been done by missionary organizations (such as the Summer Institute of Linguistics, now known as SIL International) with an interest in translating the Christian Bible and other significant historical and religious books. As of 2009, at least a portion of the Bible had been translated into 2,508 different languages, still a long way short of the full coverage. The most extensive catalogue of the world's languages, generally taken to be as authoritative as any, is that of Ethnologue (published by SIL International), whose detailed classified list as of 2009 included 6,909 distinct languages. Nevertheless, a more updated version from 2017 claims there are 7,099 languages currently spoken today. We cannot however be entirely sure of the correct number as there are too many people all over the world speaking their own local dialects. It is though expected that this number should decrease soon, as of today only 23 idioms already account for half of the world's population.

Popular Language Families

In this book I will not be informing you about all the current language families in existance – as it would take quite a long time! Instead we will take a look into the families that surround these 23 most spoken languages. If you do not hear about a particular language here do not worry! This only means the language does not have a number of speakers considered high enough to be mentioned here.

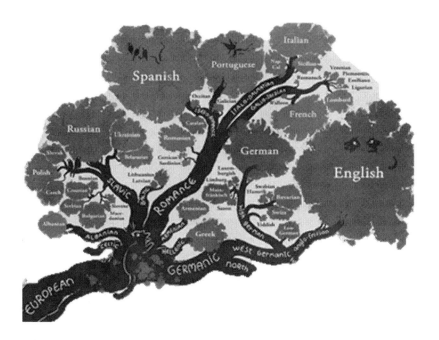

Figure 1. 2 European language families

Indo-European

The Romantic language family members (sometimes called the Romanic languages, Latin languages, or Neo-Latin languages) are the modern languages that evolved from vulgar Latin between the sixth and ninth centuries and form therefore a branch of the Italic languages within the Indo-European language family. Today, around 800 million people are native speakers worldwide, mainly in Europe, Africa and the Americas. The main languages from this group are **Spanish** (410 million speakers), **Portuguese** (250 million), **French** (80 million), **Italian** (60 million) and **Romanian** (25 million).

The Germanic family is a branch of the Indo-European language family spoken natively by a population of about 500 million people mainly in North America, Oceania, Southern Africa and Europe. The West Germanic languages include the three most widely spoken languages in the group: **English** (about 400 million native speakers), **German** (over 100 million) and **Dutch** (23 million). Other major West Germanic languages are **Afrikaans**, an offshoot of Dutch, with over 7.1 million native speakers; and Low German, with roughly 6.7 million native speakers. The main North Germanic languages are **Norwegian**, **Danish**, **Swedish**, **Icelandic** and **Faroese**, that combined have a total of about 20 million speakers.

In the Slavic family, languages either use the Latin alphabet, such as Croatian for example, or the Cyrillic alphabet, like in Russian. Which alphabet they use depends on whether the national languages developed under western Catholic or Eastern Orthodox Christianity. Catholicism based in Rome, transcribed local languages in the Latin alphabet. Orthodoxy on the other hand transcribed local languages in Cyrillic alphabets, which are based on the Greek alphabet. The main Slavic languages include **Russian** (155 million speakers), **Polish** (42 million), **Ukrainian** (40 million), **Serbian** (11 million), **Czech** (11 million), **Belarussian** (9 million), **Croatian** (6.2 million) and **Slovak** (5 million). Slavic languages are spoken by more than 300 million people mostly in Eastern Europe and Asia (Siberia). All Slavic languages are believed to have descended from a common ancestor called Proto-Slavic, which, in turn, is thought to have split off from Proto-Indo-European possibly as early as 2,000 B.C. Proto-Slavic was probably the common language of all Slavs as late as the 8th or 9th century A.D. However, by the 10th century A.D. the various Slavic varieties had begun to emerge as separate languages. Mostly all Slavic languages are national or official languages of the countries where they are predominantly spoken. In addition, many of them are working languages of countries where they do not have official status. This is particularly true of Russian which is no longer an official language in certain Eastern European countries but remains an important working language of the former Soviet republics.

Another branch of the Indo-European family is called the Indo-Iranian branch. This includes both Indic languages such as **Hindi** (490 million speakers), **Bengali** (226 million), **Punjabi** (100 million) and other languages primarily spoken around South Asia, as well as **Persian** (Iranian) and **Kurdish** spoken by around 110 million people in the Middle East. In addition, other branches of Indo-European spoken in Asia include the Slavic branch, which includes Russian in Siberia; **Greek** (13 million speakers) around the Black Sea; and **Armenian** (12 million).

Sino, Altaic and Afro-Asiatic

Figure 1. 3 Indic language families

In contrast to European languages, the dialects spoken around Asia differ greatly from one another. The Sino-Tibetan family for example is composed by **Chinese Mandarin** (1.3 Billion speakers), **Burmese** (33 million) and Tibetic languages. This is a family of over 400 different languages spoken in East, Southeast and South Asia. The Altaic family has several smaller but equally important languages spoken across central and northern

Asia, such as **Korean** (77 million speakers) and **Japanese** (125 million). Languages such as **Arabic** (420 million speakers), **Hebrew** (5 million) belong to the Afro-Asiatic family. This is a large language family that comprises about 300 or so living languages and dialects, according to the Ethnologue estimate. It includes languages spoken predominantly in West Asia, North Africa, the Horn of Africa, and parts of the Sahel.

Is Chinese the same as Mandarin?

Partially.

Mandarin refers to the spoken language, just like Cantonese for example. Both Mandarin and Cantonese are dialects of the Chinese language. In fact Chinese is a language that can be spoken in many different ways, therefore the importance of knowing the difference and making sure you are choosing to learn the correct dialect. Cantonese is spoken mainly in Hong Kong while Mandarin is spoken mainly in mainland China.

The English Language – A Master Key

Since you have purchased the English version of this book, it is safe to assume that you already have a reasonable knowledge of English – thus making everything so much easier! The English language serves as a master key when it comes to unlocking vocabulary knowledge in other languages. English is a member of the Germanic family although it is linked to many European languages by descent or influence.

Figure 1. 4 The History of English

Through it's formative years, English has been strongly influenced by several other European languages through historical events such as the invasion of the Roman Empire in 43 AD, Anglo-Saxons around 450 AD, and Vikings later in 793 AD, mixed with already existing local Celtic languages.

The Romantic languages had a massive influence on English as well, with over 50% of the English Language vocabulary coming from Latin or French. In fact, when we break down all the origins of English words it can be traced back with 29% of the words coming from French and Latin each (majority related to medicine and law), 26% from Germanic languages such as Old/Middle English, Old Norse and Dutch, and 15% coming from other languages.

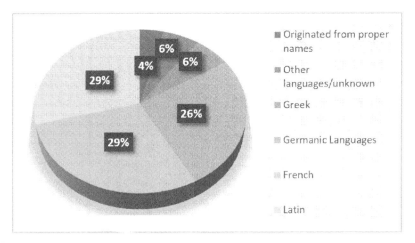

Figure 1. 5 Origins of the English language

According to languages specialists, and based in parts with my own experience, there are a few languages that are definitely easier to learn if you already have a good enough knowledge of English. This might be a criteria worth considering when choosing your language of choice. It is always better to begin with something easier and progress later on to something more complex. Here are a few of the languages considered to be easier to learn if you already know english:

Norwegian, Danish, Swedish and **Dutch** – After all they are members of the Germanic family just like English! This means they share quite a bit of vocabulary i.e. sommer and summer. Norwegian is officially the "easiest" of the group in this case. With its straight forward grammar, Norwegian has only one form of each verb per tense. There is also a certain similarity with it's words as in "Kan du hjelpe meg?" meaning "Can you help me?", in both languages the sentence structure and words order remains the same. Danish has a much quicker and softer speaking pattern than Norwegian, with a more difficult pronunciation overall. Nevertheless it is still flatter and more monotonous than English, with a grammar considered to be easy and somewhat alike. Danish also has similar words that can be easily identified for an English speaker such as Mandag (Monday), Tirsdag (Tuesday) etc. Swedish also has a quite similar syntax to English. Verb formation also has parallel patterns, making the pronunciation the hardest part of the learning process. The language has nine vowels and a sje-sound that is unique to Swedish. A major reason why Swedish is easier for English speakers to learn is the large number of cognates the two languages share. For example, "gräs" is grass in Swedish, and "kung" is king – two clear cognates. Like Norwegian, Swedish has relatively simple grammar rules and similar word order to English. Dutch is the final Germanic language on the list. It's the third most-spoken of them, after German and English, which does make sense since the shared vocabulary of Dutch sounds quite a lot like a combination of German and English. A really interesting characteristic of Dutch is that many words are spelled exactly the same as they are in English, more so than in almost any other language. However, use caution when learning because they're often pronounced differently. For instance, the word "rat" has the same spelling and meaning in both languages, but in Dutch it's pronounced like the English word "rot." Also, keep an eye out for false cognates, like the Dutch word wet, which actually means "law." If you stay vigilant enough, Dutch could be a great option for beginners.

Spanish, Portuguese, Italian, French and **Romanian** – The second language group that is quite easy for English speakers to learn is the Romantic family. As previously discussed in this book, English shares many words with Latin. In Spanish, cognates such as "correcto" (correct) and "delicioso" (delicious) makes this language definitely a good option. The pronunciation is also fairly easy and straightforward, with most words being pronounced exactly as they are spelled. Grammar wise it becomes slightly more confusing, specially with the different feminine and masculine gender words that are not found in English. Nevertheless the easy accessibility of Spanish, the official language of no less than 20 countries, also facilitates the overall learning process. Portuguese, just like Spanish, also shares a large number of cognates with English. However, be careful with the false cognates i.e. if you ask for a "pasta" you will be receiving a folder! The pronunciation might also be a problem in the beginning due to its often used nasal sound when pronouncing words like mãe (mother), não (no) and mão (hand). Grammatically, it is very similar to all other Romantic languages, however with less prepositions than English, just be careful not to mix things up when creating a sentence! Italian, though not as widely spoken as Spanish or Portuguese, has strong latin roots that allow for a sizeable quantity of cognates such as "errore" (error) and "problema" (problem). Another plus is the fact of how the language is pronounced just as it is written, considered as an easy language to read. Grammatically speaking, Italian follows the standard Romantic family structure, with gendered nouns and parallel order of words. Italian also has the advantage of having fewer verb forms than French or Spanish. French on the other hand, is the hardest to pronounce amongst all Romantic languages, with its vowel sound and silent letters. The easiest thing about this language is the large common vocabulary with English, with words such as royal and fiancee. French also has gender nouns and more verb forms than English – 17 against 12. Lastly, we have Romanian that is perhaps the most interesting of all languages in the group, as it is definitely the hardest to learn. It is said to be the most similar to Latin, with 80% of it's structure based on it, although it also has had a Slavic influence on its vocabulary. In Romanian, articles might be slightly confusing for the average English native speaker, as it adds the definite articles as a suffix at the end of nouns i.e. *frate/fratele* (brother/the brother), while indefinite articles appear before nouns *copil/un copil*, (child/a child). With a reasonable number of cognates, it should still be considered an option for someone who also wishes to learn a Slavic language in the future.

Indonesian – For those looking to lean towards the Asian language families, this is a good option to start with. It's alphabet uses Latin letters, with a phonetic system where words are pronounced exactly as written. The grammatical structure however is quite different from English, with a lack of rules, verb conjugation and grammatical genders, the language also lacks in the plural form (words are then repeated twice) which can all be quite confusing at first. A great option for those who have difficulties with grammar rules.

Key Summary Points

This is by no means guarantee that learning any of the languages mentioned above will be easy. However, it definitely helps to start with something that isn't that far from a tongue you already master. In my personal experience, learning English before any other language definitely made it easier to learn the rest.

➤ The world is filled with thousands of different languages but the reality is that only a few dozens of them have a relevant enough population that speaks it.

➤ Half of the world's population speaks only 23 different languages.

➤ Languages belong to different families that are divided based on language structure, origins and word similarities.

➤ English is the master key for languages due to the influence of several different languages families through history.

➤ Many languages, specially from the Romantic and Germanic families, are therefore easier to learn for those who are already fluent English.

Chapter II

EASIER SAID THAN DONE

"Continuous effort – not strength or intelligence –
is the key to unlocking our potential."
- Winston Churchill

I am sure you have already heard somewhere that it is much easier for children to learn a new language than for adults. This is for the most part true. However, new evidence about the brain shows us something quite different. In this chapter, I will be introducing you to what makes the brain of an infant more susceptible to a new language. We will also be taking a look into the long asked question if it really is easier for children to learn a foreign language. The environment in which a child grows up has a lot to say when determining one's ability to communicate. It will determine how the child perceives language, how it learns to speak. Since I was a toddler, I remember my mother constantly correcting me when speaking with her. She always ensured I spoke the most correctly possible Portuguese, something she inherited from my grandfather. Because of this I have always learned my own language quite well since early age. The ever so constant addition of Italian words and expressions from my grandmothers, and the random day trips to Paraguay and Argentina have added to my first years an opening into different cultures and their own languages. I wish back then I would have grown up speaking two languages fluently, however that only happened at age 15 when I moved to North America. Most of the languages I speak today I have actually only learnt after adolescence where my brain was already almost completely developed. There is hope for each and every one of us to learn a foreign language, no matter the age. It is indeed much easier for some people to learn than others, the same way some people can do mathematics much better. In my case, I never had the highest grades in the science department (unless it was biology, of course) but I definitely did my best at subjects such as history, literature, languages, and well biology (it's all about reading.) People who enjoy activities such as reading, writing, debating, giving speeches have definitely an advantage when it comes to learning languages. Whatever it is that you are good at, you are fully capable of learning a language on your own. This book, was written to help even the least skilled of people that still wish to learn another language in a decent enough level to be considered fluent.

The Role of The Environment

Social conditions, from the country of birth, financial situation, education and etc, have a massive influence in the opportunities people have to learn a language and their attitude towards it. For example, learning it while you respect and are respected by the native speakers of that language have a completely different impact than when learning it by suffering any sort of hostility from native speakers, or when you hold negative feelings towards the culture or country in question. This unfortunately tends to happen in certain degrees with youngsters who adventure themselves into exchange programs at early age. I myself have experienced this while learning one of my languages. Although I will not mention which one nor the country where I was based, but it did have a massive impact on my learning capabilities. I felt as if they had been drastically decreased, as this language in particular when compared to others, took the longest for my brain to fully accept.

Another external factor to be taken into account, is the overall contribution a learner receives. This meaning, the "samples" of language the learner is exposed to. It is impossible to learn a language without some sort of external input. As each person has different levels of difficulty when it comes to learning, some might do better with the aid of a tutor while others will prefer a more independent form of dealing with the language such as through chatting with native speakers for example. Something to look for and identify before you take on any language is to think if you would do better by learning it from an input that has been simplified to you (as if you were attending classes for example) or by dealing with a direct authentic approach (such as moving into the country in question). So, if your goal is to learn a language you "don't really like" or have any sort of "trauma" from, you might want to re-consider what you're doing. Not saying it's not possible, just saying it would be *harder* to learn a language you already have negative feelings towards.

Part of the method I have used to become multilingual, and is what I have based this entire book on, is trying to bring the language's environment into your own. Here are a few suggestions on how you can also do that, no matter where you are in the world.

Become Like a Sponge

This is probably the best advice I will ever give you. Become an *active* sponge. Absorb every part of it but move quickly as well. Listen to it, speak it, sing, it, write it, read it. When it comes to learning a new language from scratch, everything is permitted. Now, alright, how exactly would you do that? When you move into a different country, it becomes quite easy since everywhere you go you have access to the language. However, for most people this isn't really the case. So how can you do it? It's the simple things. For example, you can switch the settings language on your mobile for the language you're currently learning. This way you will be forced to read it every single day. Change the language settings on your social media profile, follow news pages, listen in the form of music when you go to work or to university and when you are touring the city inside the car or the bus. Need some background noise to carry on some tasks around the house? Put some series or videos in that particular language. Every moment you have try to use it for learning purposes. You can learn from everything!

Engage With Native Speakers

The world has just about 7 billion humans living on it today. With advancements in technology, one can move from one side of the world to the other in less than a day. It is then impossible (unless you live in a hut somewhere in Siberia) to not have got in touch at some point in your life with people from different countries. There is absolutely no better way to learn a new language than to practice communication skills with native speakers. Let's say, you live in a small town and the only foreigners you see speak languages you have no interest on, how to proceed? For starters, the internet is a beautiful and magical place. You can communicate with people from all over the world, either by texting and online chatting or making use of video calls and direct calls. Social media is definitely a powerful tool in this process. There are so many ways anyone can find pages and groups on Facebook or Instagram in the respective language they wish to learn, where there are tons of native speakers just waiting for someone to chat with. The whole point of this chapter is to inform you how important it is to adapt your environment to the language if you truly wish to learn it. If you can manage to find a person who is a native speaker of your desired language, this is the chance for you to go on and start a new and exciting friendship. Begin by chatting the basics, ask for help! If this is not the case, internet will always be there for you. Just remember, it is crucial at some point throughout your learning process (preferably half way through it) that you are able to communicate with native speakers. Only then you can be truly sure you are on the right track.

Embrace The Culture

This is in my opinion one of the funnest parts of learning a new language. When it comes about embracing the culture, I mean *fully* embracing it, one can be as creative as one wishes to be. For example, this is your chance to learn how to cook a delicious typical dish from the home country you wish to speak the language from. Maybe you might even have to translate a few food names, or perhaps getting in touch with their culture by trying a traditional dish will change your perspective on their way of living. No one can tell what will come from it, but it is definitely part of the cultural embracing phase. This include things not only like food but music, literature, movies, art and everything else that belongs to the culture or country in question. Maybe you are lucky enough that your city hosts different cultural events (a popular practice around major cities in Europe) where you get to experience all the elements mentioned above without ever having to go too far away from home! Obviously, if you happen to have the opportunity to travel to different places, maybe this is the time to consider a two weeks get away of pure language immersion and fun (highly recommend you take a trip like this by yourself, if you wish to learn anything!). This is another interesting aspect of this process. As much as I encourage you to build all sorts of relationships with native speakers, you should be strongly considering spending more of your time on your own. The reason for this can be purely described in one word: focus. Unless you and your best buddy decided to learn a language together (which I only recommend if both parties are strongly motivated to do so), it might be best to cancel out on some social gatherings, as this would only distract you. In the case of travelling in order to learn the language, doing so alone will basically force you to communicate with others, thus improving the chances you will actually learn anything.

Do Children Really Have It Easier?

It is commonly believed that the ability to learn languages declines as one becomes older. The structure of the brain is not completely formed at birth, thus a considerable amount of development continues after the child is born throughout childhood until adolescence. This entire process is called maturation and it happens at different speeds for each individual. The human brain also has a high degree of plasticity, meaning that after damage has occurred the brain can (to a certain extent) recover itself or adapt in response to change. Recent evidence has concluded that the brain is actually much more flexible during adulthood than it was previously thought. During the first few years of our lives, our brains are busy developing itself forming all the connections needed to define our personalities and who we really are. Many things can drive a child's language development, such as genes, environment and most importantly social interaction. Let's start by looking at language learning in terms of the simplest observable phenomena – what babies and young children say and how they perceive languages. Usually, during the first few months of age, children begin to develop a sort of vocalization made entirely of random sounds.

The Development of Language in Children

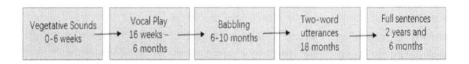

Figure 2. 1

These random sounds gradually give way after six months of age to a second language development stage refered to as "babbling", where the baby makes a large quantity of meaningless sounds that are not quite yet words. At this stage the baby is "playing" with its vocal cords and trying to imitate the sounds parents make when they speak. An experiment has been carried on in the last century by linguistic specialists Ruth Weir and Jean Aitchison in which the babbling of an American, Russian and Arabic babies were recorded and later on played to several random mothers from these three same ethnicities. The American mothers could often identify the American baby, the Russian mothers the Russian baby, and the Arab mothers the Arabic baby. However, none of them were able to distinguish between the remaining two babies. Therefore, even though the babies were not actually saying words, they were already formulating sounds that are most common in the language they are hearing around them. At this stage, a baby is capable of replicating the pronunciation of any sound in any language, thus the massive opportunity of learning. Despite the ability to learn and replicate sounds and accents much easier, it is not yet clear if children are indeed better than adults when it comes to learning a new language.

In 1983, evidences suggested that in contrast to popular opinion, adults might in fact be better than young children when learning a foreign language. Adults are much more capable to understand all the components of learning a language, specially the complicated rules. The reason why most believe that it is easier for children to learn is simply due to the exposure a child is under. This concept is similar to the idea on why it is easier for children for example to learn how to ski than for adults. The reason for that is simply because children have very little life experience and external knowledge, thus they are much more likely to put themselves at risk in order to learn how to do something. Rather than an adult will already be aware of the potential dangers of learning such as breaking an arm or a leg.

Children love new experiences and since their lives aren't nearly as busy as ours they are able to fully immerse themselves into any language. Let's say for example a couple with a small child that moves from France to Norway. For the adults speaking Norwegian will be quite uncomfortable at first (unless they already know the language) and they will mostly be speaking it with a strong sort of accent. The child on the other hand will easily become fluent with very little accent or no accent at all. This happens on the basis of what the child learns from the environment i.e. by speaking and being spoken to, and in the almost complete absence of teaching (meaning without receiving any sort of classes) and of conscious learning (the child has no idea it is learning a different language). This happens via full immersion done by the child. As mentioned several times throughout this book, the best way to learn a language is to fully embrace it as this way your conscious and unconscious brain will pic up the language much faster.

"Many wonder how I learned to speak English so fast. Growing up in the festive country of Brazil, music had always stayed close to me. Later on, I moved to America at an older age, many expected me to have a strong accent. However, due to my interest in music I exposed myself to English songs. Engaging myself with the music benefited my pronunciation tremendously. Also, because of the changing tones of the words in the songs and the emotions associated with them, made it much easier for me to distinguish between each words and to slowly pick up on their meanings."

Carla R. Corley,
Student at **Worcester State University**, Massachusetts

Key Summary Points

The main lesson to take from this chapter, is that even if you were unable to learn a second language as a child, it definitely isn't too late for you to begin today – not matter your age. If you have the chance, do teach your children as many languages as possible as this will definitely be a strong advantage as they grow up in this ever changing competitive world.

➤ It is for the most part easier for children to learn a foreign language. However, recent findings about the brain prove that even fully grown adults can just as easily pick up a second or third language.

➤ The environment has a massive impact in the learning development of both children and adults.

➤ Interacting with native speakers is crucial when learning. There are many ways to do that without ever leaving your home country.

➤ Learning a language requires complete immersion into the correct environment. Embrace the culture. Make use of food, music, movies, books, or whatever else interests you!

Chapter III

CHOOSING THE RIGHT LANGUAGE

"The limits of my language, are
the limits of my world."
- Ludwig Wittgenstein

Congratulations! You have made this far and I promise you things are about to get much more interesting! We have passed the main introduction through the world of languages, now is time to choose the one language that is right for **you.** It is time to ignore your friends suggestions to learn French because it sounds fancy, or Spanish because it makes you look sexy. This is the time for you to take a break and think – what language interests me the most? I have prepared a brief guide that will help you choose the right language for all your needs. As believe me, when it comes to the rough times of learning a new language on your own, this will make all the difference between failing and succeeding.

Ask Yourself The Right Questions

More or less like everything else that is important in our lives, this requires a lot of thinking and questioning before anything actually gets done. Let's think for a second, who actually are you? Behind the social profiles we have built in order to hide ourselves from the world, this is the time to be truly naked, truly honest with yourself. Before I chose to learn each of the languages I speak today (except obviously for my native one), I always asked myself a few important questions. There were also times where I tried to learn a language for no real reason, and the result failed miserably simply because during the hard times (there will be many) I had no real logic behind my motivation, causing me to simply give up.

So, before going after all the trouble of trying to learn a new language on your own, take the time to ask yourself the following 8 questions:

1) **Where do I wish to be 5 years from now?** *(This book offers a method of learning that is centered in one's way of life. If the language you wish to learn has nothing to do with your future plans it might be time to reconsider and find a more suitable option.)*

2) **How can a foreign language help me to get there?** *(Knowing a foreign language will open many doors in your life, so it is time to think which doors exactly you wish to be opened.)*

3) **What cultures interest me the most?** *(Idioms play a huge part in different cultures. Liking a culture in particular can definitely be a big push in motivation.)*

4) **What is my ability to face challenges?** *(Do I prefer to do things in the easier or harder mode? Some languages will require much more from you than others.)*

5) **How much effort and time am I willing to put into this?** *(What exactly are my priorities in life and how much of my day am I willing to adapt for this new language?)*

6) **What language attracts me the most and why?** *(Something to consider are the major aspects of the language. Does the sound of someone speaking it sounds pleasing to you? It definitely should! Think of as many attributes as you can.)*

7) **How much would I be willing to live in a country where my language of choice is natively spoken?** *(If you can not stand the idea*

of living in the country where the language is spoken, not even for a few weeks, then this may not be the language for you.)

8) **What is my incentive to learn this language?** *(Are you looking to learn this language for work, travel or just for the sake of it? This will make a huge difference down the line!)*

Hopefully by this point you have already selected a few languages you have in mind. If not, close this book and take your time to carefully answer each one of these questions until you have a clear idea about which language you wish to learn. Now, I would like to ask of you that in the end you choose one language only – as trying to learn two or more at the same time will only confuse your brain. Once you have reached a higher stage and have already learned a couple of new languages feel free to try and learn as many more as you can all at once (it's actually more fun than it sounds).

Best Languages (in my opinion) to Learn Today

Before anything I would like to make clear that the following list is based entirely on my opinion and research conducted, however it is not an official published list. Politics, economics and travelling are three of my favourite activities which has lead me on years of research and personal development experiences in order to identify how I could improve my chances of building a strong career as quickly as possible. For those looking to do just the same, this is your list.

It is nearly impossible to claim that a particular language is more important than other. Nevertheless when looking upon which languages are the most influential ones in the world today, I have created a list of the languages I believe should be learned in order to strongly benefit you in the work place within the next few years. Obviously several factors should be taken into account such as what matters to you and what are your priorities. If you dream of becoming the next wolf of wall street or a volunteer in different parts of the world, your language priorities will shift. Nevertheless, at the end of the day, we can all agree on how some languages are more important to know than others due to political influences, number of native speakers worldwide, countries currently speaking it and so on. Let's take a look at seven of the languages that in my opinion, you should be thinking about learning if your priorities are career and travel related.

English – Of course, what has become almost the universal language of today, English is definitely a must know nowadays. English is spoken by no less than 50 countries totalling almost 400 million native speakers around the world. Not just that, in the list of most influential countries in the world, places like the UK and the USA always make to the top of the list, making English the must have language for those looking to achieve academic and professional success, specially in the business world.

Chinese Mandarin – The language spoken in the most populated country in the world, Chinese is definitely the language one should be looking to learn for the future. China has already taken over the USA as the most powerful country and the prediction is for their power to keep increasing in partnership with other important countries. About one sixth of the world's population has Chinese as it's first language. Many companies in the UK today are looking for people with any level of Chinese skills.

Spanish – This is definitely the one Romantic language you should be learning right now. Spanish is spoken in 20 countries all across South and Central America, as well as Europe and North America. For those interested in travelling, Spanish is the language to go for. It can also be quite useful in matters of business and career wise since more and more developing countries that speak Spanish keep on expanding and their influence will be greatly felt in the years to come.

Arabic – Unnecessary to say, Arabic is the language for those with political and economical interests towards the Middle East. Arabic is spoken in 22 countries by around 420 million people. The language has a strong influence in religious matters as it is directly linked to Islam and it's traditions. The Middle East has been a place of high importance in the past decade, with places like Dubai and Abu Dabi being known for their vast population of millionaires. As oil and natural gas continue to be powerful commodities, this language is definitely worth learning.

Russian – For those into politics, it is no hidden fact the large influence Russia has been having recently. The country itself is the 9th most populated in the world besides its language being spoken in several countries across Europe that used to belong to USSR. With the largest land size on earth, Russia will remain a powerful player in the world politics for the years to come. Besides, with the country's economy regaining power and with sanctions soon to be lifted, speaking the Russian language will be a powerful asset when conducting business with Eastern Europe.

German – When we look at Europe, German stands out as the official language of the strongest and most stable economy in the block, Germany. It is easy to see why since the country has the largest population in Western Europe and is located at a very strategic position, right in the heart of Europe. Cities like Frankfurt enjoy a massive influence in the financial world specially into the banking industry. German is also the official language of Switzerland and Austria, two of the most developed countries in Europe with one of the highest life qualities in the world. The language therefore is a powerfull tool when dealing with business within the EU, as well as handy when exploring the beautiful alps.

Portuguese – The official language in the largest South American country, Portuguese has over 220 million native speakers, and about

260 million total speakers in 10 different countries spread around the Americas, Europe and Africa. Definitely a language worth learning for those looking to travel, as there are records of people even speaking it all the way over in India. With the creation of BRICS, countries like Brazil have become increasingly more important inside international economics due to it's massive population, the fifth largest in the world.

There are many other languages I would like to be discussing its importance here. Nevertheless these are definitely the ones to consider if you are interested in pursuing a political or international business career. Obviously, knowing such languages is a powerful asset also when travelling, due to it's popularity and large number of native speakers. However, just travelling should not be your priority when choosing a language, unless of course travelling is part of your job.

It is easy sometimes to get carried away by the thought of learning a language just because we wish to visit a particular country, when at the end of the day our financial situation plays a massive role in our daily decisions. Therefore, think carefully about how the language you are hoping to learn today could become an asset in the near future. The figure above, is definitely one of my favourites, as it shows quite well the importance of the seven languages I have recommended by the number of native speakers.

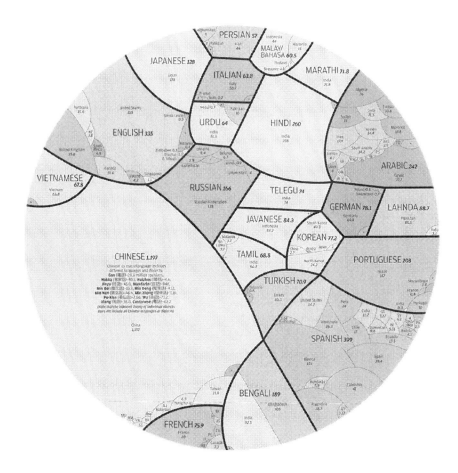

Figure 3. 1 Most spoken languages around the world

Key Summary Points

➤ Choosing the language you wish to learn carefully based on your life plans and needs is the best approach. This will keep you motivated throughout the tough times you will encounter during the learning process.

➤ Asking yourself the right questions before making a final choice will help you to weight on what's truly important to you.

➤ There are a few languages that are quite important to know today specially when it comes to certain career paths such as business and politics. English and Spanish may sound like obvious choices to most of us but more Eastern languages such as Russian and Chinese will be quite important in the years to come.

Chapter IV

THE BILINGUAL BRAIN

"One language sets you in a corridor for life.
Two languages open every door along the way."
- Frank Smith

If a person is fluent in two languages, then he or she is considered to be bilingual. The common image of a bilingual person today is of someone brought up in a culture where they are exposed to two different languages early on in life. In order for this definition to be correct it is not entirely necessary for someone to be equally fluent in both languages, as long as there is enough competence for communication in both of them. Some people happen to be trilingual or just multilingual overall, which causes this definition to become a little vague since people vary on the interpretation of the word "fluent". Being bilingual is actually quite ordinary in certain parts of the world such as Wales (Welsh and English), Canada (French and English) and many other places with reasonable sized minorities groups living within a country.

Human Brain – The Most Complex Thing in The Universe

It is common knowledge that the brain controls muscular activity in the human body. It is clear that the brain is also the seat of conscious thought. Indeed we can all agree that when we have an idea, we make the unconscious decision to convey it in a language form and subsequently actually produce some utterance in the speaking form, where the brain is involved at every step along the way. The exact process of the brain's meditation between our thoughts and our linguistic expression of them is still not yet completely understood. As already mentioned earlier, our brains are like "plastic" thus meaning they are able to re-shape itself in certain conditions. This is called Neuroplasticity or Brain Plasticity which refers to the brain's ability to change throughout our lives. The human brain has the incredible skill to re-build itself by forming brand new connections between brain cells i.e. neurons. This Neuroplasticity happens in three distinct cases; firstly, during the beginning of our lives as our brains go through an intense developing stage. Secondly, in cases of brain injuries in order to preserve vital functions; and thirdly, whenever something new – such as a foreign language – is learnt. Many experts argue today that one can "teach" it's brain to learn better and faster, by simply changing one's daily habits. Things such as exercising for example, or eating a healthy diet, reading, and learning another language stimulate the brain in different ways. There is no guarantee that what is currently known today about the brain will remain the same in the coming years. An organ so complex, experts spend years arguing about how it works and every now and then another major discovery is done that changes completely how we see our brains. Nonetheless, if there is something no one doubts about the brain, is that it has indeed a certain level of plasticity that can alter one's learning capabilities and even one's personality. This varies from person to person, although it is great to know that there is hope for all of us grown ups to re-shape our brains into becoming sharp in any possible language.

Two vs One – The Advantages of a Multilingual Brain

Since making of English my first and prior language, I have

noticed within myself several changes into my way of thinking and into my overall behaviour. Making decisions suddenly became a more logical process while expressing myself through words became much more easier. Several studies show that people who use a second language to make important decisions have much better chances to make the most rational and correct choice. It is no question that knowing two languages is a massive advantage in many ways, no matter which are the languages you know.

Figure 4. 1 Brain activity in bilingual brains

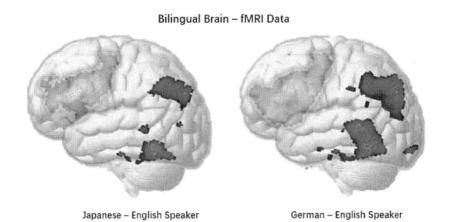

Bilingual Brain – fMRI Data

Japanese – English Speaker   German – English Speaker

The same brain activity has been reported in general bilingual individuals, independently of the languages used.

As the figure above indicates, there is no difference between which languages are spoken and their particular effects on the brain. Therefore, whichever language you choose to learn will increase your brain activity the same way as any other language, regardless of its complexity. The benefits of learning a second language are plenty, ranging from all sorts of changes in one's brain and personality. Here is a list of a few of the many advantages of learning a second or third or fourth language.

A Healthier Brain

Learning a foreign language is like learning an entire new system with distinct rules, etymology and meanings. This learning process forces the brain into recognising an entire new structure, which isn't the easiest of tasks. As the brain works out the meanings and makes full use of this new arsenal to express ideas, it sharpens its skills on reading, negotiating and problem-solving.

Several studies have been carried on regarding Alzheimer and dementia within the brain, with consistent results showing a positive correlation between learning a foreign language and postponing age problems linked to the brain. For monolingual adults, the average age for first signs of dementia is 71 years, while for adults that speak two or more languages the average age spikes up to 75 years, showing a significant advantage. These studies considered factors such as education and income level, gender and physical health.

Memory Improvement

You don't need to be a neurologist to agree that the more your brain is used, the better it functions. Learning an entire new language structure involves familiarizing oneself with similar vocabulary words and rules from your native or previous languages. Applying such information into communicating with others forces your memory to work harder thus becoming stronger. Educators and specialists like to define the brain as if it were a muscle, since it functions better the more it is exercised. The exercise of remembering words means that multilingual people are better at remembering sequences and lists. According to studies carried on within the field, bilinguals and polyglots are better at retaining peoples names, directions and overall lists.

Become Smarter

The process of learning a new language boosts your memory and prevents your brain from dementia and alzheimer for longer. This is because the functionality of the brain significantly improves. This obviously plays a major role in making the brain sharper thus making you smarter. Based on school standardised tests, kids who spoke a second language had substantial higher scores, particularly in maths and reading, when compared to their monolingual peers. It is not just about scoring higher in school tests, but also about how much keener the mind becomes in the way that the brain becomes better in spotting things that are irrelevant or deceptive. Cognitive skills are greatly developed and results are usually seen by the learner itself once the second language is already part of the thinking done by the brain. Other areas that are improved are the ones in charge of executive function and attention, regardless of the language learnt. Increased IQ is one of the proved benefits of knowing a second or third language.

Better Decision-Making and Multi-Tasking Skills

The decision-making skills becomes greater in multilingual people. Besides having to learn new vocabulary and rules, there are nuances and vernacular expressions that someone who is learning a new language must frequently pay attention on and be able to judge what is appropriate to use and what isn't, as well as look out for hidden and double meanings. This, causes the decision-making process to become more prudent and discriminating, which comes in handy when making any sort of important decision. It is also said that making a crucial choice in a second language causes you to take longer to decide as the brain works harder to process the entire decision, thus forcing you to becoming more rational before making any final choice. Bilingual individuals are shown to be more logical and rational, as well as more perceptive and aware of their surroundings.

Multi-tasking also becomes noticeably easier. This has been noted especially with bilingual children, and how quickly they manage to switch between two systems of speech, writing and structure.

According to a study from the Pennsylvania State University, this language switching skill makes these children better multi-taskers. In one study, participants used a driving simulator while doing separate and distracting tasks as the same time. The research found that people who spoke two languages or more made fewer mistakes while driving.

Build Your Creativity and Self-Confidence

By choosing to learn a new language you are telling yourself "yes, I can". This must become your new motto throughout this entire hard and satisfying process. As with any skills that are mastered, confidence increases, and learning a new language is no different. The techniques used to develop a second language result in a greater sense of openness of the mind. Self-confidence is a natural consequence after summing all benefits of learning a new language. By simply mastering one skill, the other faculties in the brain are developed. People tend to gravitate around multilingual people more as many find that polyglots have an open mind and are seen as confident and interesting people.

Creativity also suffers a relevant impact on the matter. Researchers around the world have concluded that multilingual speakers are more creative than monolingual ones. Learning a foreign language improves not only confidence, problem solving skills and multi-tasking, but also forces you to experience with different words and cultures. This has a positive impact on your sense of creativity. Leveling up second language skills leads you to situations where sometimes you are unable to remember certain words, thus having to improvise with what you already know. It improves your skills in divergent thinking, which is the ability to identify multiple solutions to a single problem.

Become Richer

Does learning a foreign language makes you richer? Maybe. If you are motivated enough. The reasoning behind this is that the more languages you know, the more attractive you look inside the work market. Your resume will stand from the crowd and companies will be more likely to hire you. Knowing more than one language means doing business with different countries, which could lead to promotions or paid work abroad. It also offers a great chance to do some extra money on the sides by working as a translator. In my case, it opened the doors to becoming the interpreter of Manchester United first team players at age 19.

"I have worked closely with employers for 25 years and helped to set up and manage over 2,000 student placements during this period. It is difficult to exaggerate the benefit for students of being confident to talk in more than one language. Not only can it provide great practical assistance to business, but it demonstrates adaptability and empathy towards other cultures which is of such broad relevance and value."

Chris Procter,

Senior lecturer at the University of Salford, United Kingdom

With universal unemployment problems, a multilingual ability is definitely a competitive edge over others. It is an ability that tells of one's intelligence, flexibility, openness to different cultures, and better decision-making skills. Potential employers consider this a valuable asset in an employee's skill set, as they-re able to connect with a broader range of people and carry on activities internationally. In this new age of start-ups, companies are increasingly breaking into new markets. You naturally increase your personal and professional value if you are able to negotiate with manufacturers in another country or communicate with customers who don't speak your native tongue.

"English was essential and instrumental in the development of my career. It was because of the language knowledge that I was able to first get my first opportunity to work on international projects in Brazil, with American and European clients in multinationals such as Accenture and Capgemini. Learning English has also made it easier for me to move abroad. At many points in my career, English was more relevant and had more weight to when it came to work opportunities than having an university degree."

Guilherme Schneider,
Digital Strategist in London, United Kingdom.

Make More Out of Your Trips

Imagine how much easier it will be to travel to certain places just by knowing another language. Ordering food, asking for directions, talking to locals and many other things can be simplified only by knowing a few sentences already. Austrian philosopher Ludwig Wittgenstein is credited with saying that "the limits of your language are the limits of your world," and he was absolutely right. Knowing two languages or more opens up your vacation destination possibilities. Fluency isn't even required, locals anywhere appreciate that you have taken the time to at least attempt to learn and communicate in their native tongue. This shows a greater level of respect and is an easy way to meet new people. Also, getting to a comfortable speaking level in a foreign language is a great motivator to get you out there practicing and meeting new people.

Another thing to consider, is how in some places locals try to fool tourists simply because it is much easier than fooling locals, specially when it comes to pricing. In places such as my dear home country Brazil, people try these tricks all the time and often succeed in obtaining a few extra bucks from naïve tourists. Therefore knowing the local language can help you avoid being scammed.

Second Language Acquisition

By this point in the book I am hoping you are already convinced of the many advantages that come with the learning of a new language. Second language acquisition is something that is different to each and everyone of us. While for some it might be clearly easier, one must remember that everyone has equal chances when taking into account the fact that our brains continue to re-shape itself even after a certain age. There are a few methods that are seen as ways of learning a different language, although there isn't any one that is proven to be the most effective of all. Each method works better with a certain language and with certain types of people. As it can be seen in the picture below, only one of them makes reference to learning a language inside a classroom, while the others focus on the importance of interaction with the language and with natives speakers. Although most people today believe the best way to learn is by enrolling themselves into a paid course, the main point of this book is to focus on how there are many other approaches that are better and much cheaper. While I believe the methods of submersion and immersion are definitely the best ones, for some the security of learning inside a classroom with the guidance of a teacher might just be overall better. This highly depends on the individual in question. Based on my experience, enrolling in language classes was the biggest waste of time and money, as no matter how much the teacher tried explaining something I just could not get it.

Figure 4. 2

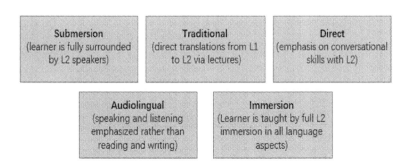

Methods Used to Learn a Second Language

The figure above shows five of the best methods to learn a second language that are recognised by linguistics and psychologists with expertise in the area. I have briefly already spoken about the Submersion method and it's true effectiveness. However, this method mostly works with people who are either by choice or necessity moved to a foreign land and must therefore adapt. This book is written based on the Immersion method and how it can be applied to the busiest of individuals entirely on their own.

Key Summary Points

➤ The human brain is quite a complex organ. It has a plasticity that allows it to change itself according to our environment and experiences regardless of age.

➤ The language you wish to learn makes no difference when it comes to changes in the cognitive functions of the brain. All languages affect the same areas in the brain in similar ways,

➤ Being multilingual has many advantages such as a healthier brain, memory improvement, increase in intelligence levels, better decision making and multi tasking skills, increase in overall creativity and self confidence, payment raise, and better quality trips among many others not mentioned here.

➤ There are 5 known methods of language acquisition and each one of them works better according to the individuals's situation and preferences. Immersion is in my opinion the most effective of them.

Chapter V

THINKING IN ANOTHER LANGUAGE

"Cogito ergo sum – To think is to be"
- Rene Descartes

"A different language is a different version of life"
- Federico Fellini

Thinking is undoubtedly completely intertwined with language. And thinking in another language is quite a tough task. The biggest mistake that someone could make when trying to learn a foreign language, is to directly translate things into their own native tongue. This only causes a temporary memorization of a phrase or expression. A language must be trully understood in order to be learned. One must speak with feelings instead of merely repeating words. In this chapter, I will be explaining how any person no matter the age or background can shape's their brains to accommodate any new language, and what are the best approaches in order to accomplish it.

In my method of choice when studying each of my languages, I have learned to read and write along with listening and speaking it all at the same time. I strongly believe this is key to quickly re-shaping your brain into creating a place to accommodate a whole storage of words, rules and sounds that were never there before. As previously seen in Chapter II humans tend to learn foreign languages better until the age of puberty, as the brain goes through a whole state of development that begins during childhood and extends through adolescence, it adapts to new things much easier than during a post-developed phase. Once the average person has reached it's 20's years mark, there is no more major brain development to be done. Yet the human brain is perhaps the most fascinating thing in the universe, and continuous development and changes are possible all through a person's life. The key of course, is to do the same thing as toddlers when it comes to learning, and fully implement all the major elements of the language into our daily routines. In this chapter, I will be guiding you as best as I can throughout this engagement and adaptation process.

Language and Thought

Through the past one hundred years, psychologists all over the world have tried to identify and explain the deep relationship between language and thought. The question of "does the language I speak influence the way I think or is it the other way around?" is a difficult one to explain since the brain itself is the most complex of all existing organs. When we look into the animal world, it is easy to see how animals communicate and think in a straight forward way without relying much on any sort of language whatsoever, thus suggesting that language itself cannot be essential for problem solving nor thought. During the beginning of the last century, early approaches taken to examine the relations between language and thinking led specialists to believe that thought was nothing more than speech, whereas the thinking process is nothing more than a series of muscle contractions that produce speech. This has been strongly argued throughout the 20th century, to the point that in 1947 a group of scientists carried on a series of experiments on volunteers where they temporally paralyzed their muscles while obliging them to solve all sorts of problems inside their heads. Despite all volunteers being unable to make any use of their muscles, they were still able to fully think and solve problems, thus proving there is much more behind the act of thinking than just moving the vocal cords and muscles. According to the Russian psychologist Lev Vygotsky (1934/1962), the relation between thoughts and language is one of enormous complexity. In a different experiment carried on in 1958 by two linguistic specialists in the United States, children that were native speakers of English and Navajo were subjected through a series of tests in order to prove the cognitive consequences of grammatical differences in diverse languages. It was observed that due to the Navajo's language dependence on the shape of objects, endings to words such as "carry" for example vary depending on the object being handled. This led the scientists to conclude that children who were native Navajo speakers would group objects in a different way when compared to children that were English native speakers. As all children were bilingual, the study based itself in two groups with those who were more Navajo-dominant into one and those were more English-dominant into another one. As predicted by the experiment leaders, the group of Navajo-dominant children did indeed group objects in a different way that focused more on form than colour, in contrast to the English-dominant children. An example that supports the results encountered in this experiment, is that English speakers use the subjunctive mood to easily encode counter-factuals such as "If I had gone to school I would have met with my friends". Languages such as Chinese for example to not have a subjunctive mood. Therefore native Chinese speakers find it harder to reason counter-factually which can be attributed to the lack of subjunctive mood in the language, therefore to a great extent influencing their thoughts. This is because the form of the construction needed for counter-factual reasoning is longer than the English subjunctive. Their memories are therefore much more easily overloaded than of those who are native speakers of languages that do support this form. A second example that bring forward this belief is that although English does not mark grammatical gender, many other languages do. In Portuguese for example there are female and male nouns, while German has female, male and neutral forms. In 2005, four linguistics from the University College of London found that the effect of gender on thought were highly constrained. Meaning that the difference of genders in languages does not have any significant impact. The results show a small difference in the verbalization of animals for example (it has no effect on objects) when compared to those who are native of a three gender language or no gender at all. Nevertheless, such experiments shows us that the languages we speak can indeed affect our way of thinking and our performance on language related tasks. In the end, the cultural element also has an impact on how we perceive the connection between language and thought. In the Western hemisphere of the world for example, it is assumed that language and inner speech assist thinking; in the Eastern side on the other hand it is assumed that talking interferes with thinking. Such cultural differences may affect performance to a certain degree. Thinking out loud for example was found to be helpful with European and Americans, while for Asians it was not beneficial at all. Perhaps the main conclusion we can make about how language and thought are connected is that there is definitely a relationship between them, although this relationship is extremely complex. Both our environment and biology combined have a mutual effect in determining our basic cognitive structure. In the end, the cultural element also has an impact in how we perceive the connection between language and thought. Thinking in another language after childhood years is a great mission that has the power to change the way we think and perceive the world. There is really no other way of becoming fully fluent unless you can master the art of thinking in a certain language.

SIDE NOTE

Pay attention to dreams in a foreign language, this means the subconscious part of your brain is adapting to it and the thinking process should become much easier!

Four Main Components

Since the main goal here is think in your language of choice, there is no better way of accomplishing that, than combining all the components of learning, thus creating a sort of complete immersion without leaving the comfort of your home.

English testing systems all over the world such as IELTS and TOEFL (required for international students to test their language skills before enrolling in an English speaking higher institution) base their grading criteria on four points – Listening, Reading, Writing and

Speaking. The key method in this book is to introduce all these four systems of learning into daily habits that we already have. Before analyzing such components, I would like to make it clear that there are many books available to purchase online or in book shops that are accompanied by CDs where the student can practice all the four components on their own simmultaniously. I definitely recommend the use of such books and if you do have the chance make sure to take some time to select the best ones as not all of them offer an easy to understand learning approach. However, it is still possible to learn on your own just as efficiently without them. Let's look into the importance of each of these components when learning a language and how we can make good use of them throughout our busy lives. To help you deal with these components I have prepared a list of tips followed by two scales that range from 1 to 5 in levels of complexity and effectiveness, based on my personal experience and results obtained from trial and error.

Complexity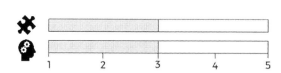

Effectiveness

Complexity: This measures the levels of difficult involved in executing this task entirely on your own.

Effectiveness: This informs how effective the method is during the learning process.

Listening

Listening is the most important part of learning any language. If you can listen and understand what other people are saying, you are pretty much sorted. Obviously, listening has a massive role to play in every step of learning any language. As I know from experience, it is quite desincouraging to try to listen and understand a foreign language for the first time even if you already have some knowledge in it. Do not panic about it – we have all been there! I can confidently say this is one of the hardest parts of learning. How do you teach your brain that new sounds mean new things? What if you go to a place where people speak in a different accent? The best thing to do, is to keep your ears busy with the new language in question, trying to mix as much as possible content with accents from different countries while at the same type keeping some order, making sure you don't confuse your brain. Music, films, series all can be quite helpful at this stage. Try to incorporate the language on a daily basis, perhaps instead of watching your favourite series in your native tongue you could opt to view a dubbed version with subtitles. This way you will be associating the words you hear to the words you read and already know. Also, by listening to songs you like in whichever language, you can get your brain used to the words and accents much quicker. It will also (hopefully) make you curious enough to check the lyrics translation and perhaps learn some new vocabulary words! My best tips for acing the listening part of the learning process are:

Series, TV Shows and Movies

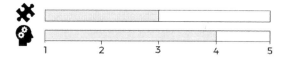

We have all been guilty of watching for a second or third time our favourite series and TV shows. This is one of the best methods of learning to understand the spoken language, by re-watching your favourite TV-shows over and over again. Make use of subtitles at first but feel free to ditch them when you feel confident enough. While

Netflix is perhaps the most popular streaming platform currently available, others such as Amazon Prime Video, Hulu, and standard cable TV companies also offer the same services and opportunities. It's all a matter of using whichever one is more convenient to you. Movies are a fantastic way of learning as well. Looking for national movies is a great option as it not only offers you the opportunity to hear the language been locally spoken, it also offers great insights into the culture of the people and their country. Another good option is to re-watch your favourite films dubbed in the language you wish to learn, or make use of subtitles in a language you already understand (just be careful not to spend the whole movie reading the subtitles instead of trying to understand what is being said!). Sometimes, just having a series or movie running in the background while you get other things done can already be quite useful. Remember, your brain learns things both consciously and unconsciously.

Find Songs You Love

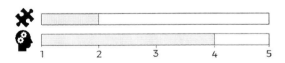

We all have that one song we cannot understand and yet it has the most amazing beat. Find a few more and listen to them on a constant basis. Try to see if you can pick up any words and feel free to use the lyrics as an opportunity to learn new vocabulary and phrases. The main problem some people might find with this is the fact that songs in a language we do not understand tend to be quite intimidating and therefore desincouraging at first. Do not let that stop you, in my experience listening to music has made my ears much sharper when trying to understand a conversation. As you will see, music plays a huge part in helping the process of self teaching a language. The best approach to this is to find several songs you enjoy and play them over and over until you see signs of improvement. Also, do not feel embarassed in trying to sing a few parts of the song every now and then. Afterall, this is an efficient way to improve your pronunciation as well as listening skills (read the *Speaking* part to find out more about this). Before every event where I had to translate Hispanic football players, I would always listen to only Spanish songs during my commute to work. I might be slightly off track here but even being already mostly fluent just listening to the songs made me twice as confident with the language.

Youtube is a Powerful (and free) Tool

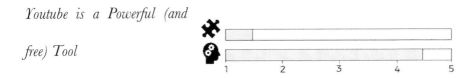

The beauty of internet nowadays is the ridiculous amount of free learning material we have available at our fingertips. With Youtube, you are able to directly watch news, adverts, trailers, series and many other videos made in foreign countries in all possible languages. Make sure to make great use of it! A busy and stressful day after work could be a great excuse to watch funny Youtube videos – in your new learning language, of course. Besides all the fun you can have while learning, there are also plenty of useful short video lessons that can help you at the beginning with basic phrases and words. In my case, I have used Youtube to a great extent in order to watch local news and presidential speeches when learning a few of my languages. The platform is easy to use and it has over 100 hours worth of video uploaded every single minute – that's a lot of content you can make good use of when learning! Youtube is also a great way to hear different accents from native speakers without ever leaving the comfort of your home.

Reading

Reading is more or less a completely different system for each language. Obviously if you already speak English and are looking to learn a Romantic or even Germanic language, this won't be much of a challenge since both language groups use our dear Latin letters, making it somewhat easy to learn how to read. However, if you are in for a challenge, this part is perhaps the most exciting one. Learning how to *properly* read in a foreign language that uses a different alphabet, such as Russian, Greek or Arabic for example, is a tough task. The reality is most people will simply give up once they try to read a simple sentence. The first thing you have to understand though, is that for a large amount of people, these letter are the letters in which their brains process everything around their lives. And what you should be asking yourself right now is, if this many people can read such different looking characters, why can't I as well?

With reading there is really no mystery to it. The key is to keep a few words here and there spread through your daily tasks. Independent of the language, the process is entirely the same. The only thing that changes is, once again, how much effort you are willing to put as obviously languages with different alphabets require extra time and focus. Another issue with reading, and this is true no matter the language you are looking to learn, is the enunciation of written words. In languages such as English or French, words are pronounced quite differently from how they are written thus making it difficult for non native speakers to get the reading out loud part right. This involves lots of practice and unfortunately lots of time memorizing how each word is spoken. My best tips for acing the reading part of the learning process are:

Start With The ABC

Before you go and try to read anything, take a look into the language's alphabet. Take your time to learn how to pronounce each letter (Youtube videos are great for this) just so you are able to read whatever word outloud, even if you have no idea what it means. For those learning language with Latin letters, you might feel over confident and think you can still ace the reading whatever it is. However, trust me, there will be moments you will be quite confused so I recommend doing this step before anything. For those looking to learn a language with a different set of letters, this is not only necessary as it is absolutely crucial. Most languages have letters that represent certain sounds that do not exist in English, therefore learning them one by one is key. Take your time to study how each letter looks and how it can be somewhat "associated" to English letters, which will make things much easier in the beginning and later on.

Make Use of Social Media

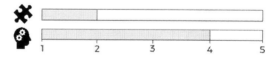

No generation has been as addicted to social media as we have. For most of us it became almost a ritual to check our Facebook, Twitter, Snapchat and Instragram profiles on a daily basis, to the point where it is the last thing we check before falling asleep and the first thing we check after waking up. Since social media is such a massive part of our lives, and they do not seem to be disappearing anytime soon, why not make the best out of it? Following pages with content in the language you wish to learn might not seem like a huge step forward, however trust me, it really is. Think about all those moments where you're lost in time scrolling down through your newsfeed and all the senseless things you are reading. Think how useful it would be if you could use this time and energy to learn another language. It's the simple things really, looking at a funny meme or interesting article in a different language, how would you react to that? In truth, unfortunately, most people will just continue scrolling down until they see something in a language they can understand. It is always easier to ignore what we don't know and run right back to our comfort zone. If you are that kind of person, this isn't the book for you. My hope here is that you will be curious enough to find out what that meme or article are saying, and stop what you are doing in order to translate the words you don't already know. And just like that, you have already learned something – which literally took you less than a couple of minutes.

Post-It Notes

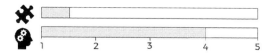

Alright, despite our constant need to interact with others and maintain a decent social life, we still spend a reasonable amount of time inside our homes. In the comfort of our own countries we take for granted how important it is to know the name of the simplest of things. This technique, I believe, is a common one amongst exchange students. You simply write the name of things as they are, i.e. fridge, lamp, bed, in the language you wish to learn and place them over the respective item. This way everytime you look at it you will think of the word on that language. Sounds like something quite simple, yet it is extremely useful besides the facts it is absolutely free and takes almost no time to have it done.

Read a Book

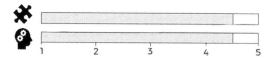

Books are without question one of the best sources of learning that exist. Reading an entire book in a different language might seem like a massive challenge but it is the final test when it comes to practicing your reading abilities. I suggest leaving this step towards the end of your learning process when you already feel confident enough. It will definitely not be an easy task but I guarantee by the time you finish you will feel much more confident on your language skills.

Writing

Letters are the basic units of any written language. There is much more variability in the structure of written languages than there is in spoken languages. Whereas all spoken languages make use of a basic distinction between consonants and vowels, there is no such common thread to the world's main written languages. The learning approach to writing is quite similar to reading. Except this time it requires a bit more effort. Writing is one of the ways to ensure something is engraved into our memories. The act of writing something down has been scientifically proven to ease memory thus facilitating remembering things. With a language it is no different, there are so many words we need to learn and writing them down definitely makes the whole process much easier. The writing part, such as in reading, will depend highly on the kind of language you wish to learn. For example, if you wish to learn a language that has a Cyrillic alphabet such as Russian, you will first learn how to understand each character or letter which will be much more complicated than going for a Latin alphabet based Language. Now, before anything, let's make it clear that writing involves two different aspects: cursive and non cursive. Again, this all goes back to those initial eight questions I recommended you ask yourself before choosing a language. In the case of Russian, it's cursive form is extremely hard for non native speakers to learn it. It's many curves and different shapes make it very difficult since the letters you see typed in a computer or printed in a book look much different from the letters you would have to write down. Nevertheless, regardless of which language you choose to learn, make sure you reserve some of your time to practice writing of important sentences or words. Here are some useful tips to improve your writing skills with a foreign language:

Understand The Lyrics

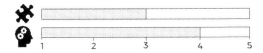

It is no surprise how much we love to hear songs and how deep some of the lyrics can be. I have already mentioned of the benefits of listening to music when learning earlier on in this chapter, and now I am back to the topic to help you a bit further this time with writing. One of my favourite approaches to help remembering how to write certain words and to practice writing in a different alphabet, was to select the lyrics of a song I enjoyed and just copy them down line by line until my hands begin to hurt. This not only engraves the words deeper in my brain as I write them but also brought my Russian cursive to a whole new level. Also, this is a great way to better understand what the lyrics mean – take the chance to translate word by word if you must!

Practice

Your Calligraphy

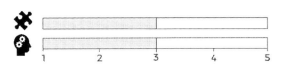

During my child years back in Brazil, learning how to properly write in the cursive way was the law. Therefore we always had in our backpacks our calligraphy notebooks where we would write the same letter over and over again until it is perfect. This repetition method is quite useful special for non latin alphabets. It might sound boring at first but you will see for yourself the feeling of acomplhishment should come at the end of each sentence!

Remember how I mentioned the utility of these colourful post notes during the reading learning process? Well it is just as useful when it comes to writing. Perhaps you found a nice quote you enjoyed while scrolling through social media (Remember to follow pages on your language of choice!) and would like to remember it word by word. Keeping some notes around your house or office will offer you a daily reminder of your learning goals. Motivational quotes are the best in this case!

Conjugate The Verbs

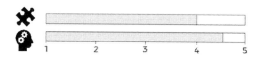

This is an extremely important part of the entire language learning process. Ok, before you are able to do anything with the language you are trying to learn, you must by all means know about it's main verbs and how to conjugate them in the many forms. English is relatively easy in this aspect but the reality is most languages alter the ending of the verb to adjust it to the form it is being spoken. During my initial learning periods for Russian and Spanish I spent a great amount of time writing all conjugating forms of the 50 most important verbs in the language, This has been extremely helpful specially when it comes to pushing the boundaries of your memory and ensuring all this large amount of words gets to be correctly remembered.

Speaking

Alas, perhaps the most exciting part about learning a new language! For some speaking proves to be the easiest part, while for others it is just the hardest. This has a great deal to do with pronunciation as each language has its own unique sounds. Another difficult part is being able to create complete and correct sentences in your head fast enough so you can replicate them through speech. For most people this proves to be a massive challenge. In my point of view one can only dream of speaking in a foreign language once that language has already penetrated one's brain − thus leading to the person thinking into the desired language. It is rather impossible to formulate and speak in sentences where your brain is unable to rationalize in the language in question. The biggest mistake beginners do when learning is trying to translate everything they are trying to say word by word. This will certainly fail almost every single time as languages have different syntaxes where creating a sentence in Portuguese will be completely different than a sentence in German. While most Slavic languages for example make use of the to be verb such as in English, Russian does not have the need for that. Therefore, translating word by word the sentence *ya sam doma* (I am home) from Croatian to English would make perfect sence as the subject "I" exists followed by the to be "am" or "sam" and finished with a location "home" all within the same syntax. However, if this was to be translated to Russian, the person would say *ya doma* only without the need of the Russian equivalent "to be" word, thus leading a direct word by word translation to be directly wrong. Therefore, when dealing with the speaking part one must be very careful as sometimes the misuse or mispronunciation of a word can have serious repercussions. As a German teacher I once had always said, whenever you attempt to speak in whatever new language you are learning, stick to the words and phrases you already know instead of trying to make up something new. Here are some more tips (these ones are mine though) on how to improve your speaking skills:

Chatting with Natives

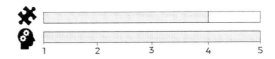

I can't stress enough how important it is to somehow get in touch with a native speaker of the desired language. By talking to them you will most likely be corrected when pronouncing words incorrectly besides having the opportunity of learning it first hand how to speak in certain ways be that slang wise or formal. If you are lucky enough, you might find a few foreigners within your town or much easily done in a great city. If you have the chance to do so, try making as many new friendships as you can with native speakers and use the chance to practice your language skills with them. Most of the times they will be thrilled to hear a foreigner speak in their language, even if it's filled with grammatical mistakes! You can also learn a lot about their culture and society, in any words it's probably the most effective way of learning how to speak in another language. Cities with large student communities usually have chat groups filled with international besides an infinite number of societies around campus. For those who do not have this opportunity locally, there is always the power of the internet, where anyone can chat with anyone else literally anywhere in the world. Make use of online chat platforms or interact with others on social media, just try to talk to them as

Google Translator is Your Friend

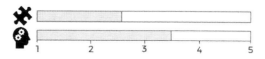

Let's forget for a second all these interpretation and grammatical mistakes made by Google Translate. Afterall, it's easy to forget that this is a software and not a human. This online free of charge

translating tool can be quite useful when it comes to learning how to pronounce certain words. When something is translated in the webpage you get the option to listen to the word or sentence as many times as you wish just by clicking the little volume button on the top left corner. This comes in quite handy when you have no access to a native speaker (although it should not by any means be considered as a reliable replacement but only as extra assistance).

Sing It

You will be surprised with how much the simple act of singing over a song can help you with pronunciation and with overall speaking skills. If you can manage to mimic the exact sound for each word, you brain will more easily adapt when the switch between languages being spoken happens inside your head. Also, if you feel confortable singing it you will also, hopefully, feel comfortable enough while speaking it!

Key Summary Points

When it comes to mastering these four major language aspects there is really no secret other than focusing and placing some of your time into small tasks that added together will eventually lead to a decent amount of knowledge of whichever language you wish to learn. By this point I hope you are already certain of which language suits you best and already have a pretty good idea of how you can fit the learning process into your routine. In the following chapter, I will be talking about my personal experience and the tricks I've used to learn each one of my seven languages.

➢ Thinking in a different language is the only way to guarantee you have fully learnt it.

➢ There are 4 main components to consider when learning how to think in any language. These are Listening, Reading, Writing and Speaking.

➢ Each component has its difficulties. However, it is perfectly possible to learn how to master them on your own without ever having to go anywhere!

Chapter VI

SIX LANGUAGES IN SIX YEARS

"Learning a foreign language not only reveals how other societies think and feel, what they have experienced and value, and how they express themselves, it also provides a cultural mittor in which we can more clearly see our own society"
- Chancellor Edward Lee Gorsuch

The title of the book, 7 languages in 7 years is a brief way to summarise what my life has been like since I left my home country 6 years ago. As a native speaker of Portuguese, that was really the only language I grew up with, besides every now and then a few random words in Italian that were thrown around by my grandparents. Other than that, I had an ordinary monolingual childhood and was in fact the worst student in English class during my school years. By the time I landed in the United States for my high school exchange in August 2011 at age 15, I could barely speak a word in English. The initial two months I remember, were the hardest ones. I was unable to communicate properly and people would make fun of my language skills a lot. By the third month, I was already fluent and had managed to take the SATs (the American university exam) where I scored better than the average American student, specially in the English subject. Now when I look back, I understand that my fast learning of English was due to two main things. First, I had been forced to learn the language by being in full immersion, as that was the only way I could communicate with the world. And second, I spent many many hours watching over and over again my favourite series at the time, Friends. I will get into more details about that later. While going through this learning process, I also took the time to teach myself Italian. As I began my studies in America, I took a few Spanish lessons which helped me regarding the grammar issues, however the real learning came during my years of work at Manchester United F.C and Foundation. As as volunteer from Volunteer 99 project, I mentioned my knowledge of the Spanish language. When asked if I could upon short notice interview and translate two of their most powerful players at the time, I quickly accepted. These two weeks that followed in February 2015 (at 19 years old) I spent every single second of every minute and every hour listening to Spanish accents from Argentina and Spain (the countries of origin of the players) and conjugating verbs, reading books, learning in every way I could. This opened the way for a career of English and Spanish translations that completely changed my life. Back to the languages, upon arrival in Britain, I created a series of relationships based in the Russian language. Constant exposure and hours of work opened my brain to this language, causing myself to question everything I believed on prom political ideals to religious belief. Later on in September 2015 I took on a scholarship to study my second year of my bachelors course in Mainz, Germany. This led the way into my understanding of German. . Today, I work on teaching myself Chinese Mandarin through books, Youtube videos, online sources and the great supply of language books available at University of Salford's library. Whenever I have the chance, I exchange a few words with my Chinese speaking colleagues and friends, always looking for feedback and to practice. In this chapter. I will be explaining in details how I've learned each one of my languages, and will give you some useful tips so you can learn it on your own as well!

Learning English

How can I begin talking about the language that has changed every single aspect of my life? English became my number one language. The one I use for important issues, when sorting problems, during negotiations, speeches and everything else. After all that is the language I felt comfortable enough to write my first book with! English is probably the easiest of all languages to learn in terms of grammar, vocabulary, rules and etc. And also because, English has a little bit of every language in its composition as you've seen in Chapter 1. Since you have purchases the English version of this book, it is safe to assume you're your English is fluent enough. However, even English has it's more complex forms and academically speaking there is always room for improvement. If you feel confident enough, feel free to skip to the next language! Learning it on your own nowadays can be extremely easy. Since English is everywhere from movies to videogames I trust this to be an easy and fun process. If you are reading this book however, means you already have enough knowledge on the language. With this Language, the way I learned was through full immersion as I had no other choice since everyone around me only spoke English. This definitely is the most efficient way of learning however is not the only one as I will be explaining throughout the next languages. Nevertheless, here are my main tips for learning English on your own:

Documentaries are your friends – I have already spoken quite a lot about series and movies (and will be speaking about it much more throughout this chapter) but I find documentaries to be a much more powerful tool when it comes to learning. If your aim is to study let's say to be a veterinarian for example, watching Animal Planet and National Geographic documentaries will help you learn relevant vocabulary that you otherwise would not have access to from simple standard movies or TV shows. Channels such as BBC also offer a massive variety of informative series from all possible topics. Once again it is all down to why you wish to learn English for.

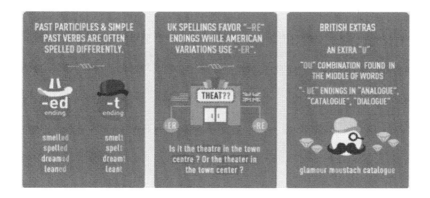

Figure 6.1 US vs UK Spelling Differences

The world of TV series – The amount of television series seen by millions of people has increased drastically. There are plenty of options to choose from. They not only reflect situations that may mirror our lives, but also offer interesting storylines and characters. During my years in North America I basically perfected my English skills by watching a very popular 90's sitcom called Friends. Initially, I was not able to understand much and that definitely frustrated me. During my second week in the USA, I was brought to the local Wallmart by my American family, where I purchases a mini portable DVD and all the 10 seasons of the sitcom. Since my host family had no TV and I had no laptop, I thought this to be the best way to learn. As soon as I would have some time for myself, I would watch the series over and over again until the point I could understand everything that was being spoken. English, today, is my first and main language. I could not imagine myself having to do business in Portuguese and afterall the first book I have ever written in my life is in English. The language has taken over my thoughts, my ideas, my dreams. After such an intense and short term learning process, I feel almost as if my brain had been widely stretched like a rubber, becoming much more flexible to other languages as well. This series offered me an insight into the daily spoken language of average Americans. Based on this, I built my primary English base structure. Later on, in Britain, I have encountered a range of completely different accents that have changed my way of speaking and understanding the Englsih language. Even after six years using English on a daily basis for everything, I have encountered a significant level of improvement by simply watching Downton Abbey, for example. It helped me through the process of writing this book as it presented my brain with different forms and words of English I did not yet know. What was meant to be simple entertainment, became a fantastic way of learning.

British or American? –It might not seem much of a difference for native speakers, however for first time learners it can come across as slightly confusing. When I first arrived in Britain after years studying in the USA making use of academic English, I was unable to understand locals around the country especially in Manchester. For starters, everytime I asked "where is the trash can?" everyone looked at me confused until they understood what I really meant was to ask for the "rubbish bin". England and America have quite a few vocabulary differences besides the way on how some words are written, such as "color" in America and "colour" in Britain for example.

The UK itself has the largest variety of accents in such a small area per square meters in the world. Do not get me started on Scotland really, their English is something else. Cities like Glasgow have quite a strong accent that outsiders have a hard time understanding. After years having English as my first language, I visited Glasgow where I was shocked on how I was completely unable to understand a word the locals were saying. Therefore, this distinction is something important to take into account. If you learn the American English for example you will definitely have a hard time when using your language skills in Britain. Unless of course English is already your first language. If you wish to stay on the safe side, learn the British English first as it is the most formal one. This is mostly true when it comes to academic purposes, if you are looking to study in the USA for example then obviously your should be focusing on learning their English. However, I would suggest listening to as many accents possible while learning. Both the UK and the USA have a massive variety of films, TV shows and series therefore this should definitely not be a problem!

FUN TIP

Type "Glaswegian accent" on Youtube and prepare to be amazed and not understand a single word of English!

9gag – Yes, you read that right. As a big fan of 9gag myself, I could not have failed to notices how important this social platform is to learn English. Available in several places such as a website, Facebook page of mobile app, 9gag merges tons of funny "memes" that youngsters love to read. Since these memes include all sorts of jokes, this is fantastic method to introduce your brain to the Language. Since it is most of the times something funny, your brain is more likely to pic up words and expressions.

Learning Portuguese

For this language, I do not have much to say really since I was born speaking it! Although somewhat similar to it's cousins from the Romantic family (specially Spanish) Portuguese has its own sounds and its own accents. The language itself is not difficult to learn but slightly confusing. Some words have many meanings while other words the only difference between them is how strongly you pronounce the "r" for example as in "caro" (expensive) and "carro" (car). Another thing to consider when learning this language, is where exactly you want to use it. Portuguese is spoken in 8 different countries but majorly in Portugal and Brazil. In Brazil itself there are several types of accents that are quite different from each other. Just in case, make sure you learn the formal side of the language first before adventuring yourself into the slangs (as we indeed have tons of them, one for each state in the country!) Perhaps the hardest sound you will find to pronounce is the nasal "ã" that is present in many common words such as "mãe, mão, maçã. Feijão" and can be difficult for first time learners. The secret is to start by making a long pronunciation until you get the hang of it! Here are some other tips to learn Portuguese on your own:

Watch Novelas – Brazilians are in love with something called Novelas. These are the country's soap operas that last between 8 to 11 months and portray dramatic life situations and are a fantastic way for someone to learn the language. During the day, there are about 3 or 4 different Novelas streaming in the country's main TV channel, although they can also be seen online.

Consider paying a visit– Back to what I was saying earlier, the reason behind why you are learning the language is very important here. For those looking to live or work in Portugal, I suggest you don't mix their Portuguese with the Brazilian Portuguese at least for the beginning part. Independent of which country you wish to learn the language from, travelling is a great option. Brazil is relatively cheap compared to European destinations and offers fantastic views anywhere you look. Since not many locals know any language besides Portuguese, this is the best option really when if you wish to put what you know into practice.

Make good use of the Brazilian humor – It is no secret that us Brazilians love to make fun of ourselves and laugh at our own problems. A simple search on Youtube will already bring you several examples of funny videos done by locals from all over the country. Even throughout the national public TV channels anyone can find the most amusing things to watch. This comes in very handy as it makes learning much more fun, as well as offering a great opportunity to compare and contrast the different dialects and accents spoken around the country. Youtube channels such as *Porta dos Fundos* and *Parafernalha* offer a great amount of free streaming short videos that are guaranteed to make you laugh out loud.

Turma da Mônica – These are comic books sold all over the country since the 1970's and they are extremely popular among kids and youngsters. The comics are colourful and easy to read. They are filled with jokes and often make cultural references. The language used is quite easy to understand and it's a great way to practice your Portuguese reading skills.

Figure 6. 2 Turma da Monica comic strip

Learning Spanish

Spanish actually comes across as quite similar to Portuguese. When learning this language, it only took me a few days to grasp the entirety of grammatical rules and verb conjugation. The way I see it, Spanish might not be as hard to learn as Portuguese although still more difficult to learn than English. It is almost as if the language was somewhere in between. While still containing gender articles, it does not have nearly the same amount of rules and accents as Portuguese does. The tricky thing about Spanish is how different the pronunciation sounds in each of it's native countries. People from Spain will also prefer to use a more formal way of speaking rather than South American countries. A great thing about this language though is how easy it is to find native speakers to chat with. During my exchange year in America I had the opportunity to take Spanish classes at my local high school. This was the only time I can safely say that I did learn bits of the language inside the classroom, but this was due uniquely to my teacher's style of teaching. She mixed all the four main components into each section making full immersion unavoidable. When it comes to learning Spanish, it was quite easy for me due to the similarities towards Portuguese as well as English. Vocabulary wise the language is not so complicated and anyone with English knowledge should have an easier time when learning this particular language. Here are my main tips for learning Spanish on your own:

Learn your verbs – The thing about Spanish, is that if you know how to conjugate properly everything will become much easier. The writing is not really difficult and can be easily learnt from the beginning. From early on, conjugate on your own the most common verbs in their different forms. You can begin with the 50 most popular, everyday at any moment you can do a couple or a few, gradually learning and improving.

Despacito – Slowly yes, although I'm refering to the famous song that has taken over all radio stations for the past few months. Spanish is quite a popular language for music with Latin hits taking over the top spots quicker than wildfire spreading through a dry forest. This is mostly because Latin songs have an upbeat rhythm that is easy to dance to besides good looking singers such as Shakira and Enrique Inglesias that are hard to ignore. Not only that, Latin songs are the light of the party and a major success inside nightclubs all over the world. Before each of my translation events with football players at Manchester United, I would spend the whole way from my flat to the stadium listening to Latin songs over and over again only to keep the language fresh inside my mind. This might not seem like a big help but it definitely is. These songs are filled with catchy phrases that are easy to be picked up by people with no knowledge of the language whatsoever. If you listen to songs from Pitbul for example you will likely learn how to count in Spanish without much effort at all!

Novelas, novelas, novelas – I can't stress enough how important Novelas are within the Latin world. As I have previously spoken about them when learning Portuguese, the same can be said when learning Spanish. Mexico for example is a major exporter of telenovelas that are shown all over the world. This is really by far the best approach towards learning. Before translating Angel Di Maria and David De Gea for the first time, I spent an entire week watching a novela from Argentina in order to train my ears to what their accent is like. South American Spanish accents tend to be slightly more difficult to understand when compared to Spain, with vocab words that go back to their own native languages before the conquistadores arrived in the continent. Also, their pronunciation is slightly faster and words are less enunciated. Therefore, again, think carefully why you wish to learn Spanish and which of it's many native countries you wish to focus on. This will narrow down your options greatly and allow much more time for you to focus on what will be really helpful. Afterall, for those who are still beginners, listening to several different accents at the same time will do no good only confusing your ears instead.

Learning Russian

The first really complicated language I ever truly learned "on my own". I have been interested in Russian since my childhood years. As a child, I tried learning it on my own but failed miserably. Once I arrived in England, I began spending all my social activities surrounded by Russian speakers from different countries. As I would hang out with them on a daily basis, I always tried to absorb as much information as I could. Like a sponge (it really does work), I began picking up words and phrases, expressions and even tons of bad words (that's learning too!). This was the initial contact I had with the language. At home, I began learning on my own how to read and write, and how to conjugate the most important verbs. Russian is quite different from most languages, it is extremely complex in the way of how the it structures itself. In Russian, the possibilities are absolutely endless. Thinking becomes at the same time more complex yet simpler. Definitely the greatest two challenges for a westerner when learning this language is to think on it first of all, and secondly being able to read and write using the Cyrillic alphabet. I would say, in order to learn Russian on your own you must be quite motivated to do so. In my case, it was directly linked to my passion of politics. Here are a few of my very best tips when choosing to learn Russian on your own:

Formal or Informal? – English native speakers might have a problem here. In Russian, the second person is divided into the formal "вы" and informal "ты" both having its own form of speaking. This

can be quite confusing as it means you have to memorize all the verbs twice and know when to use each correctly. In this case, it would be wise to think which form makes more sense for you to learn first? For example, if your goal for learning Russian is simply to travel and make friends or to speak with your significant other, you might be better off focusing initially on the informal side of the language. While if your plan is to pursue a higher education in Russian or to use the language into your work environment then I recommend you begin by learning the formal way of speaking. The ultimate goal is of course to be able to fluently speak in both forms. However, we do not wish to overload the brain specially at the beginning, considering how confusing the Russian language can be for non native speakers.

Adapting to the Cyrillic alphabet – When it comes to reading and writing, a different looking alphabet is definitely a challenge. It has a few extra letters although most of them can be compared to the Latin ones except for minor changes. As it can be seen from Figure 5. 1, the Russian cursive may seem like a total nightmare however it only takes a few days of practice to master it. Before you attempt to do all these crazy loops and turns, you should consider beginning by writing the letters down over and over again in the typing way you see for example in the computer or in documents. The letters are shaped differently but they are much easier to identify than the cursive style. Do not be concerned if you feel that things are moving slow. Adapting to a different writing system can be complicated but it must not be rushed. Once you feel confident enough you can move to the cursive style – it helps a lot if you already use cursive when writing in your native language. By practicing the writing, you will begin to identify the letters much faster when reading. When you least expect you will be reading them just like Latin letters!

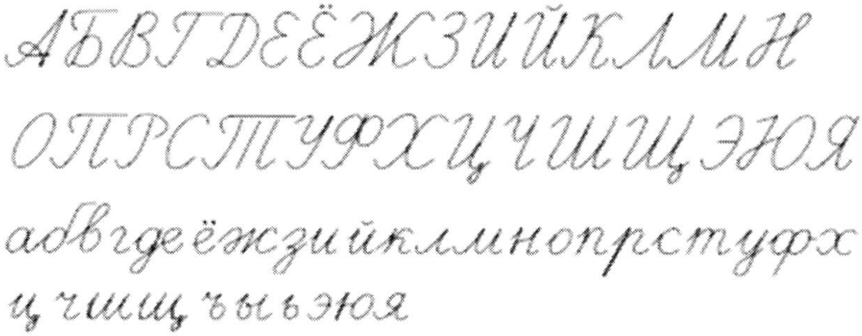

АБВГДЕЁЖЗИЙКЛМН ОПРСТУФХЦЧШЩ ЭЮЯ абвгде ёжзийклмнопрстуфх ц чшщ ъ ыь э юя

Figure 6. 3 Russian cursive letters

Listen to Vladimir Putin – This might seem like a political advice however it goes far beyond of simple world politics. I don't mean to listen to his views and ideologies but instead to listen to his Russian. Although I am quite a political person myself, this is just a very good advice for those looking to learn Russian specially for work linked purposes. Have you ever watched one of Vladimir Putin's speeches? Besides making countless jokes, he speaks in a very formal and clear manner, without ever mumbling and with a clear enunciation of the words. For beginners and intermediates, listening to his speeches is a fantastic way to sharpen your listening skills. Besides, you will also have the chance to learn quite a lot about the Russian culture by seeing how he interacts with the people and the media.

Masha and the Bear – This is a very popular Russian cartoon that was made for kids, but works just as well with adults looking to learn Russian! The cartoon is cute and since it was developed for little kids, it has a very easy language structure with common phrases and popular words being used. This is just an example of a cartoon although there are many others.

Work on the stress – Russian pronunciation is about where the stress lays. In Romantic languages for example is quite clear where the syllable with the stress is located. Yet with Russian, there is no such a thing. Of course, there are rules about how to identify such marks, but they are quite confusing for a non native speaker. In many sources online and in books it is possible to find texts where words contain stress marks making it much easier to read. Try to work on the listening and reading association exercises, such as listening to songs and reading the lyrics, or watching videos with both sound and subtitles in Russian.

Learning German

Probably one of the most difficult languages to learn grammatically speaking. German has a million rules for everything.

With it's several forms, there is an specific way to say everything. The structure in how sentences are formed is quite difficult to understand as well. On top of that, you take a look at their massive combined words and the harsh pronunciation and you are almost feeling like giving up! At least that was how I felt after the initial shock when first trying to learn German. With this language the trick is to forget all the rules for a moment, and focus on practical learning. Trying to understand all the rules at the beginning or halfway through will really only confuse you and demotivate. The first two things to understand, is firstly how to address each one of its forms and secondly how to create sentences. Like Russian, German also makes use of a formal and informal way of speaking which is pretty hard to grasp for English speakers. When it comes to creating sentences, German has very specific rules that should be followed if you wish to make any sense. Once you have all these forms and rules clearly understood in your head, is time to learn as many verbs and vocabulary as you can. It's ok if you have a hard time pronouncing the words initially. It took me one month to learn how to correctly pronounce "hören" (listen). This is all part of the beautiful journey that is to learn a language. Here are my best tips to help you learn German:

Pronunciation and Enunciation – Grammar aside, the simple act of speaking German is extremely complicated for non native speakers. The sounds in the language are quite harsh and messing up with them might cause you to go by understood when speaking with locals. Take your time to carefully learn how to pronounce each of it's letters and important words. This process should not be rushed and lots of time should be focused on at the beginning of the learning process. For this you can make use of all the tips mentioned back in Chapter 5 during the Speaking part.

Memorization – With Der, Die and Das, the best way really is to memorize the words they go with and use them as much as you can. Chances are you will be making lots of mistakes in the beginning but most of the times this won't really matter as long as you get the overall elements right. One of the tricks I found that works for most of the times with the gender articles, is that if a word is feminine in Portuguese, it will most likely be feminine in German. The same works for the masculine gender although there is nothing to be done about the neutral. Each person has it's own theory that helps them dealing with the gender articles so I suggest you find something to works for you as well. If you already speak a language with gender articles, check how they relate to German. If English is your only language, there are plenty of other tricks that work as well, you just have to find them!

Definite article (strong)

	Masculine	Neuter	Feminine	Plural
Nominative	der	das	die	die
Accusative	den	das	die	die
Dative	dem	dem	der	den
Genitive	des	des	der	der

Figure 6. 4 German definite articles

Germany? Austria? Or Switzerland? – All of these countries have significant differences regarding their accents and way of speaking. Even inside Germany itself you will be encountering dialect changes. The high and low German vary in pronunciation and many find the Swiss accent for example sounding almost like an entirely different language. Whichever is the country where you wish to learn the language from, it is important to focus on their own accent at least in the beginning to avoid major confusions.

Learning Italian

Italian is an incredible beautiful language. It is one of the best options for English speakers looking to learn a Romantic language but don't know where to start from. Pronunciation wise there is nothing too complicated about the language. In my case, Italian was the first language I ever truly attempted to learn on my own. During my years in the USA, I tried quite hard to learn Arabic using all the tips I have already mentioned on this book. The results failed miserably due to my lack of self discipline and motivation. After feeling frustrated with this attempt, I decided to teach myself first a language that was familiar and much more suited with what I was already used to. The first step for me was to understand all the main verbs and spend some time conjugating them. Verb wise the language is not complicated and it has the benefit of having plenty of words that are similar to many other languages such as English, Portuguese and Spanish. For me, the hardest part was to train my ears to listen and understand everything that was being spoken.

To sort that, I spent a long amount of hours watching to everything I could get my hands on that was spoken in Italian. As this is such a familiar language to me due to my knowledge of other Romantic languages and due to my Italian roots growing up in the South of Brazil, learning Italian on my own has proved to be a fun and interesting task. This might be more challenging for those who do not have any knowledge of other Romatic languages however, knowing English should already be enough to give you a great head start! Here are my main tips for learning Italian on your own:

Look for cognates – The Italian language is full with cognates which is a great thing when it comes to learning vocabulary. As we can see below, there are several different types of Italian-English cognates which will be quite helpful to know as you begin the learning the process.

Cognates with a different final letter

- Concerto - Concert
- Errore - Error
- Moderno - Modern
- Problema - Problem

 Cognates with a different vowel at the end

- Cura - Cure
- Nativo - Native
- Paradiso - Paradise
- Universo - Universe

Cognates that end in –ale in Italian and end in –al in English

- Artificiale - Artificial
- Finale - Final
- Naturale - Natural
- Originale - Original

Cognates that end in –bile in Italian and end in –ble in English

- Impossibile - Impossible
- Miserabile - Miserable
- Terribile- Terrible
- Responsabile - Responsible

Cognates that end in –ia in Italian and end in –y in English

- Archeologia - Archaeology
- Democrazia - Democracy
- Lotteria - Lottery
- Melodia-Melody

These are a few popular examples although many more exist. My recommendation is that you make a list with as many cognates as you can and try to find ways to remember them. Making use of the post it notes around the house is a great way of doing that!

Terra Nostra – This one might make more sense for Brazilians reading the book although it's the principle that counts. Terra Nostra is a Brazilian novela created in the 90's where it portrays the arrival of

Italian immigrants in the south of Brazil. Originally, the novela was created in Portuguese but due to it's success with the Italian people it has then been dubbed in the Italian language and is now available on Youtube. I usually don't recommend watching a series from Youtuve however in this case you can find pretty much all the *capitulos* available. There are plenty of Italian made TV shows and movies however I do like this one quite a lot since it merges both the Italian and Brazilian cultures together. The whole point of this is to find whatever suits you bets that you can watch and listen to the language on a regular basis.

Cook your way up – This might seem rather obvious although I find that most people don't even think about it. It is an universal truth that Italians cook some of the most amazing dishes in the world. Why not adventure yourself in the kitchen and try to follow original Italian recipes? You will be surprised with how much you can learn from that. It is important to mix the boring parts of learning a language i.e. conjugating verbs, learning grammatical rules, with the fun and interesting parts and cooking is definitely a great way to do that.

Learning Chinese

Everytime I tell people I am teaching myself Chinese they look at me as If I was completely crazy. It seems to me that Westerners feel more intimidated with this language than they should. Chinese is extremely complicated that is true. However, it is no more difficult to learn than Russian on German. In fact, the syntax and language structure are far easier to comprehend than in Russian, and the grammatical rules of Chinese are much simpler than German. So why aren't more people just learning Chinese? The catch of the language is in two parts – first, the pronunciation is seriously difficult due to it's complex sounds and four different intonations that could mean completely different things just by a tiny difference in the pronunciation. Second, the writing system. Chinese writing is composed by over 50,000 characters which makes it almost impossible for anyone to learn in adulthood from scratch. However, when it comes to Chinese I would say that the most important thing anyone should be focusing on is how to speak and understand the language instead of attempting to learn how to write or read it. When I spoke of the importance of Chinese in today's world, it is mostly due to the economic and political strength of China and how this affects business relations here in Europe or in the USA. This means that more and more European and American companies are looking to trade with Chinese enterprises and customers. For this, knowing how to simply communicate with a Chinese person is already pretty useful. Since the writing system is so complex there is no sense really spending hours and hours trying to learn how to read every single character if you are unable to speak a word! Chinese is one of these languages considered to be "hard mode", nonetheless if you focus only on the speaking part it is no harder than attempting to learn German or Russian for example. Although I am only still a beginner in this language, here are my top tips for those who are crazy enough (just like me) to attempt to learn Chinese on their own:

Listening and Speaking – This is what you should really be focusing on. When learning how to pronounce key phrases, you will be better off using Latin letters to write them down. If you attempt to write them as they are in Chinese characters chances are you will forget how to pronounce them in no time. Since most learning online platforms already know this, they will mostly always provide you with the written form using Latin letters. If you base your learning like this, you will find that the syntax of the sentences is quite easy.

Break it down – For every new sentence that you learn, either be "what's your name? my name is…" make sure to break it down and try to understand why this particular word is being used here. In Chinese, a different intonation for the exact same word can mean something completely different. There are key things you need to learn, as for example the word "ma" has four different meanins (according to how you say it) but you should know that when placed at the end of a sentence it transforms it into a question, as in "ni hao" (hello) becoming "ni hao ma?" (how are you?) by simply adding the "ma" at the end. If you break this sentences down word by word you will see the logic behind as "ni" means *you* while "hao" means *good*. This is only a simple example but it is important to understand the logic of the Chinese language right during the first steps of the learning process.

The four intonations – Chinese has four different intonations that can make words completely change their meanings just by a slightly higher or lower way of pronouncing. This is probably the most difficult part of the Speaking process to learn, and it is crucial to make full use of all tools available for this. When I am learning how to pronounce a certain word, I make sure I hear it over and over again in all possible ways, via Youtube lesson videos, audio books and Google Translator (remember what I said about Google Translator being a great tool for acing your pronunciation?). Once you feel confident enough, try speaking with someone native and they will definitely be happy to help. The first time I exchanged a few words with some of my Chinese friends they were quite impressed which lifted my confidence to high level thus making me even more motivated to continue learning.

Learn to read the drawings – If you look into the origins of most Chinese characters you will see that they originated from "drawings" that are linked to the word and their actual meaning. For example, the Chinese character for *fire* resembles a burning fire while the character for *tree* reminds us of a tree. Sometimes you have to be creative in order to see this but using this technique will make learning much easier. This isn't true for all Chinese characters but it is definitely a head start when it comes to learning it on your own.

Fi gure 6. 5 Chinese characters representation

Key Summary Points

➤ Each language has it's difficulties and will demand time and focus to be learnt.

➤ Languages vary on how they can be learned and it is important to choose the method that best fits the language you wish to learn.

➤ Identify what you are best at, i.e. speaking or writing and use it as a foundation point to build your learning plan and timeline.

Chapter VII

SMART LEARNING GOALS

"You live a new life for every new language you speak. If you know only one language,
you live only once."
- Czech Proverb

Once you have chosen which language to learn and why, it is time to focus on developing several goals that will enable you to be successful in the long run. Your goals here should be SMART – stretchable, motivational, action-orientaded, realistic and time-based. This idea was first introduced inside general project management in 1981 by George T. Doran and has since then been used as a powerful organizational tool. When talking about learning a foreign language on your own, you must have consistency and a sort of plan in mind. There are several variations for the acronym SMART, but in this case we will stick with the following:

S – Stretchable: Being able to stretch your learning schedule is quite important. The goal here is to fit and adapt the learning process inside your already existing routine without disrupting any major activity.

M – Motivational: Remember what I mentioned back in chapter three? Having a powerful motivation backing your will to learn is seriously the foundation of everything. This will help you not to give up!

A – Action-orientated: Everytime you have to do something on your own, taking action is necessary fir everything. You have to be able to police and push yourself towards doing what you have to do. Don't just sit and wait, be ready for action. The more you try to learn the faster you will master the language.

R – Realistic: No matter what your final goal is, your smaller goals along the way have to be realistic and reachable. For example, as you start you can say to yourself that one month from now you wish to be able to communicate the basics of the language. This is small enough to be realistically achievable and big enough to motivate you.

T – Time-based: When planning to learn something new, you should have a pretty good time frame for each one of your tasks. For example, make a list of your activities for the week and make sure to free at least half an hour of your day to focus on one specific learning activity.

This definition will help you to be successful while teaching yourself a new language. To quote renowned American philosopher and writer Elbert Hubbard, "Many people fail in life, not for lack of ability or brains or even courage, but simply because they have never organised their energies around a goal."

Learning Timeline

Regardless of how you plan your learning schedule, it is important to have a Learning Timeline before you begin anything. There is no fixed plan for this really as each one of us has their own speed when it comes to learning and it's important not to try to take on impossible tasks. In my opinion, you should be looking to create a timeline with these four objectives in mind:

Mastering the basics – Give yourself a couple of months to go through this as it is the foundation of your language skill and the most important part. In this period you should not be concerned with being able to nicely carry on a conversation with a native or understanding everything other people are saying. Do not worry about this yet, focus instead in building a solid idea on how the language functions and it's main structures and verbs. This is the time you should be conjugating all the most important verbs over and over again until you get the hang of it. If your aim is to learn a new language within one year, you should be spending somewhere between 2 to 3 months for this initial stage.

Time to chat – By now you should already be speaking a few sentences and having a pretty good idea of how to conjugate common verbs in all forms (formal/informal and first, second and third person). This is the stage where you focus heavily on listening to the language either via videos and watching TV or via talking with native speakers. By now you should have a pretty good grasp of the reading language and able to have a basic conversation via chat.

Improve what you already know – At this point you want to focus all your time in improving what you already know instead of continuing to learn new things. By that I mean to improve on the listening, writing, reading and speaking that you already know.

Perfect the details – The final stage, it is finally time to pay attention to minor details that weren't that relevant before. This includes all the grammatical rules you chose to previously ignore, but that should now be properly learnt if you wish to become fluent. Such rules are far easier to comprehend once you already have a reasonable amount of knowledge about the language. Therefore, do not concern yourself with this during the initial stages, leave it for the final part. It is important to make sure you are aware of all rules and exceptions, even if you don't see the point in them.

Key Summary

When it comes to learning languages, there is not specific learning formula nor an exact prediction of how long it will take. Languages, like us, are living things and are constantly changing themselves. Independently of which language you with to learn, it is important to know that it won't be an easy process but I guarantee it will be quite rewarding. We have arrived at the end of this book and I truly hope that by now you have a clear idea in mind of which language you wish to learn and why. We as humans are so unique in our own ways and so different from one another, that there is no system nor model that will work for each and everyone of us. I hope that you can use this book as a sort of guide for yourself and create your own way of learning based on what suits you best. Just remember, that learning a language is not only about memorizing words and grammatical rules, it's about opening your mind to a different world, it's about becoming someone else. Be in love with the language, be in love with the entire learning process. Love and passion are the only things that motivate us to do the things we do. Be confident on yourself and in your abilities. Afterall, if you can manage to teach yourself a foreign language, there is really not much left in this world that you can't do.

Bibliography

- A.Harley, T. (2014). The Psychology of Language. 4th ed. London: Psychology Press.
- Aboutworldlanguages.com. (2017). Afro Asiatic Language Family | About World Languages. [online] Available at: http://aboutworldlanguages.com/afro-asiatic-language-family [Accessed 3 Aug. 2017].
- Anglotopia.net. (2017). Language: The Differences Between American and British English Spellings Explained. [online] Available at: http://www.anglotopia.net/british-identity/english-language/language-differences-american-british-english-spellings-explained/ [Accessed 2 Aug. 2017].
- Bored Panda. (2017). The World's Most-Spoken Languages In A Single Infographic. [online] Available at: http://www.boredpanda.com/world-languages-infographic-design-alberto-lucas-lopez/ [Accessed 7 Jul. 2017].
- BrainyQuote. (2017). Top 10 Winston Churchill Quotes. [online] Available.at:https://www.brainyquote.com/lists/authors/top_10_winston _churchill_quotes [Accessed 10 Jul. 2017].
- Chineseonthego.com. (2017). Are Chinese & Mandarin the same thing?. [online] Available at: http://chineseonthego.com/are-chinese-mandarin-the-same-thing/ [Accessed 9 Jul. 2017].
- Collinsdictionary.com. (2017). *Words from French - Word origins - Word Lover's blog - Collins Dictionary*. [online] Available at: https://www.collinsdictionary.com/word-lovers-blog/word-origins/words-from-french,9,HCB.html [Accessed 3 Aug. 2017].
- Differencebetween.net. (2017). Difference Between Chinese and Mandarin | Difference Between. [online] Available at: http://www.differencebetween.net/miscellaneous/difference-between-chinese-and-mandarin/ [Accessed 9 Jul. 2017].

- Drugabuse.gov. (2017). 2: The brain is the most complex organ in the body. [online] Available at: https://www.drugabuse.gov/publications/teaching-packets/power-science/section-i/2-brain-most-complex-organ-in-body [Accessed 21 Jul. 2017].
- Ellis, R. (2001). Instructed second language acquisition. Oxford: Blackwell Publishers.
- Ellis, R. (1991). Second language acquisition in context. New York [u.a.]: Prentice Hall.
- Encyclopedia Britannica. (2017). Germanic languages | Definition, Language Tree, & List. [online] Available at: https://www.britannica.com/topic/Germanic-languages [Accessed 3 Aug. 2017].
- Ethnologue. (2017). How many languages are there in the world?. [online] Available at: https://www.ethnologue.com/guides/how-many-languages [Accessed 4 Jul. 2017].
- Grandemange, A. (2017). *A Simple Explanation Of Chinese Characters*. [online] Blog.tutorming.com. Available at: http://blog.tutorming.com/mandarin-chinese-learning-tips/how-do-chinese-characters-work [Accessed 4 Aug. 2017].
- Jackendoff, R. (1993). Patterns in the mind. Exeter: BPCC Wheatons Ltd.
- Kroulek, A. (2017). The Top Languages to Learn in 2017. [online] K International. Available at: http://www.k-international.com/blog/learn-a-language/ [Accessed 9 Jul. 2017].
- Lyons, D. (2017). What Are The 9 Easiest Languages For English Speakers To Learn?. [online] The Babbel Magazine. Available at: https://www.babbel.com/en/magazine/easiest-languages-for-english-speakers-to-learn [Accessed 8 Jul. 2017].
- Masterrussian.com. (2017). Russian cursive letters - Learn to write Russian in cursive. [online] Available at: http://masterrussian.com/video/writing/writing-russian-cursive-
- letters.htm [Accessed 1 Aug. 2017].
- Michelon, D. (2017). Brain Plasticity: How learning changes your brain. [online] SharpBrains. Available at: https://sharpbrains.com/blog/2008/02/26/brain-plasticity-how-learning-changes-your-brain/ [Accessed 21 Jul. 2017].

- M. Williams, J. (1986). Origins of the English Language. Chicago: University of Chicago.
  Merritt, A. (2017). 9 easy languages for English speakers. [online] Matador
- Nation, I.S.P. (2001). Learning Vocabulary in Another Language. Cambridge University Press. p. 477. ISBN 0-521-80498-1.
- Network. Available at: https://matadornetwork.com/abroad/9-easy-languages-for-english-speakers-to-learn/ [Accessed 8 Jul. 2017].
- Oxford Dictionaries. (2017). Oxford Dictionaries | Our story, products, technology, and news. [online] Available at: https://www.oxforddictionaries.com/?view=uk [Accessed 8 Jul. 2017].
- Pinterest. (2017). *Deutsch.* [online] Available at: https://www.pinterest.co.uk/pin/141159769549365581/ [Accessed 4 Aug. 2017].
- Plumsite.com. (2017). Language Families of Europe. [online] Available at: http://www.plumsite.com/geoculture/eurolang.html [Accessed 7 Jul. 2017].
- Project Smart. (2017). SMART Goals. [online] Available at: https://www.projectsmart.co.uk/smart-goals.php [Accessed 2 Aug. 2017].
- R. Anderson, S. (2017). How many languages are there in the world? | Linguistic Society of America. [online] Linguisticsociety.org. Available at: https://www.linguisticsociety.org/content/how-many-languages-are-there-world [Accessed 2 Jul. 2017].
- S., S. (2017). Italian Grammar: Exploring Cognates and False Cognates. [online] Takelessons.com. Available at: http://takelessons.com/blog/italian-grammar-cognates-z09 [Accessed 8 Jul. 2017].
- Thehistoryofenglish.com. (2017). The History of English - How the English language went from an obscure Germanic dialect to a global language. [online] Available at: http://www.thehistoryofenglish.com/ [Accessed 3 Aug. 2017].
- Thompson, I. (2017). Slavic Branch | About World Languages. [online] Aboutworldlanguages.com. Available at: http://aboutworldlanguages.com/slavic-branch [Accessed 7 Jul. 2017].

- UKEssays. (2017). *The Latin Influence On English Vocabulary History Essay*. [online] Available at: https://www.ukessays.com/essays/history/the-latin-influence-on-english-vocabulary-history-essay.php [Accessed 3 Aug. 2017].
- YouTube. (2017). Porta dos Fundos. [online] Available at: https://www.youtube.com/user/portadosfundos [Accessed 31 Jul. 2017].
- YouTube. (2017). Science Bulletins: Bilingual Brain 'Switch' Found. [online] Available at: https://www.youtube.com/watch?v=Cw2riItnlEE [Accessed 31 Jul. 2017].

  A. Harley, T. (2014). The Psychology of Language. 4th ed. London: Psychology Press.

- Figure 1.1 Photo credit: Ethnologue
- Figure 1.2 Photo credit: Minna Sundberg
- Figure 1.3 Photo credit: "Minna Sundberg"
- Figure 1.4 Photo credit: "The History of English"
- Figure 2.1 Data credit: "Trevor A. Harley, The Psychology of Language"
- Figure 3.1 Photo credit: "Dovas, Bored Panda Blog"
- Figure 4.1 Data credit: "Cathy Price, University College London"
- Figure 4.2 Data credit: "Trevor A. Harley, The Psychology of Language"
- Figure 6.1 Image credit: "Grammar.net"
- Figure 6.2 Image credit: "Turma da Monica Quadrinhos"
- Figure 6.3 Image Credit "Master Russian"
- Figure 6.4 Image Credit "Art of Memory.com"
- Figure 6.5 Image Credit "TutorMing Mandarin"

22815166R00085

Printed in Great Britain
by Amazon